Renaissance & Reformation Biographies

Renaissance & Reformation Biographies

Volume 2:
L–Z

**PEGGY SAARI &
AARON SAARI,** EDITORS
Julie Carnagie, Project Editor

Detroit • New York • San Diego • San Francisco • Cleveland • New Haven, Conn. • Waterville, Maine • London • Munich

THOMSON

GALE

Renaissance and Reformation: Biographies

Peggy Saari and Aaron Saari

Project Editor
Julie L. Carnagie

Permissions
Shalice Shah-Caldwell

Imaging and Multimedia
Robert Duncan, Kelly A. Quin

Product Design
Pamela A. Galbreath

Composition
Evi Seoud

Manufacturing
Rita Wimberly

LIBRARY OF CONGRESS CATALOGING-IN-PUBLICATION DATA

Saari, Peggy.
Renaissance and Reformation : biographies / Peggy Saari and Aaron Saari.
    p. cm.
Summary: Profiles fifty people who played a significant role during the Renaissance and Reformation periods, including John Calvin, Peter Paul Rubens, Catherine de Medicis, and Johannes Kepler.
Includes bibliographical references and index.
ISBN 0-7876-5470-1 (set : hardcover : alk. paper) – ISBN
0-7876-5471-X (v. 1 : alk. paper) – ISBN 0-7876-5472-8 (v. 2 : alk. paper)
1. Europe–Biography–Juvenile literature. 2. Renaissance–Biography–Juvenile literature. 3. Reformation–Biography–Juvenile literature. [1. Europe–Biography. 2. Renaissance–Bi- ography. 3. Reformation–Biography.] I. Saari, Aaron Maurice. II. Title.
CT759 .S33 2002
940.2'1'0922–dc21
                                                                                          2001008609

Printed in the United States of America
10 9 8 7 6 5 4 3 2 1

Contents

Volume 2: L–Z

Reader's Guide

Renaissance and Reformation: Biographies presents the biographies of women and men relevant to the Renaissance and Reformation period in Europe. Among the fifty people profiled in each of the two volumes are artists, authors, religious leaders, musicians, scientists, and kings and queens who helped to define this ever-changing period in European history. Renaissance and Reformation: Biographies does not include only biographies of readily recognizable figures of the era, such as German religious leader and reformer Martin Luther, Italian artist Leonardo da Vinci, and English playwright William Shakespeare, but it also includes profiles of lesser-known people, such as Italian scholar Isotta Nogarla, the author of the first piece of feminist writing, and Jewish court official Isaac Abrabanel, who protested the persecution of Spanish Jews.

Additional features

Renaissance and Reformation: Biographies also contains short biographies of people who are in some way connected with the main biographee and sidebar boxes highlighting interesting information. More than one hundred black-and-white illustrations enliven the text, while cross-references are made to other people profiled in the two-volume set. Each entry concludes with a list of sources—including Web sites—for further information for additional study, and both volumes contain a timeline, a glossary, and a cumulative index of the people and subjects discussed in *Renaissance and Reformation: Biographies.*

Comments and suggestions

We welcome your comments on this work as well as your suggestions for topics to be featured in future editions of *Renaissance and Reformation: Biographies.* Please write: Editors, *Renaissance and Reformation: Biographies,* U•X•L, 27500 Drake Rd., Farmington Hills, MI 48331-3535; call toll-free: 1-800-877-4253; fax: 248-699-8097; or send e-mail via www.gale.com.

Timeline of Events

1327 Italian poet **Petrarch** begins writing *Canzoniere,* a series of love lyrics in which he departed from the medieval convention of seeing a woman as a spiritual symbol and depicted Laura as a real person.

1451 Italian scholar **Isotta Nogarola** writes "On the Equal and Unequal Sin of Eve and Adam," which is considered the first piece of feminist writing.

1454 German printer **Johannes Gutenberg** perfects movable type.

1458 **Margaret of Navarre**'s *Heptaméron* is published and becomes an important work of the Renaissance period.

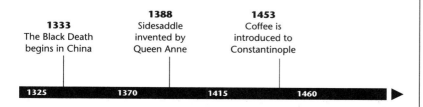

1333
The Black Death
begins in China

1388
Sidesaddle
invented by
Queen Anne

1453
Coffee is
introduced to
Constantinople

1325   1370   1415   1460

1469 Italian merchant **Lorenzo de' Medici** takes control of Florence and becomes a patron of great Renaissance artworks.

1490s German artist **Albrecht Dürer** raises woodcut to the level of high art.

1492 Jewish court official **Isaac Abrabanel** protests the Edict of Expulsion, which ordered all Jews to leave Spain.

1494 Pope **Alexander VI** issues the Treaty of Tordesillas that gives Portugal authority over Brazil.

1494 Italian preacher **Girolamo Savonarola** influences a new pro-French government in Florence.

1495 **Alexander VI** organizes the Holy League, an alliance between the Papal States, the Holy Roman Empire, Spain, Venice, and Milan against France.

1495 Italian painter **Leonardo da Vinci** begins the *Last Supper.* For this painting he experiments with oil-based paint, which is more easily blended, but his efforts are unsuccessful.

1498 Italian sculptor **Michelangelo** starts the *Pietà,* his first important commission.

1498 **Girolamo Savonarola** is executed for committing heresy, or violating church law.

1503 **Leonardo** begins work on the *Mona Lisa,* one of the most famous portraits in the Western world.

1511 Italian artist **Raphael** completes *School of Athens,* considered to be one of his greatest achievements.

1512 **Michelangelo Buonarroti** completes the decoration of the Sistine Chapel ceiling at the Vatican in Rome.

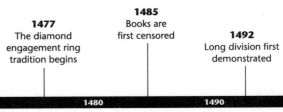

1477
The diamond engagement ring tradition begins

1485
Books are first censored

1492
Long division first demonstrated

1460   1470   1480   1490

1513   Italian diplomat **Niccolò Machiavelli** writes *The Prince,* in which he proclaims his controversial political philosophy.

1516   Dutch humanist **Desiderius Erasmus** publishes *Praise of Folly,* a satire of the Roman Catholic Church and its clergy. That same year Erasmus publishes his translation of the New Testament of the Bible, the first published Greek text.

1516   English humanist **Thomas More** publishes *Utopia.* Modeled on Plato's *Republic, Utopia* describes an imaginary land that is free of grand displays of wealth, greed, and violence.

1517   German priest **Martin Luther** posts his "Ninety-Five Theses," initiating the Protestant Reformation.

1519   King Charles I of Spain is elected Holy Roman Emperor **Charles V**, leading to the spread of the Spanish empire east from Spain to include the kingdoms of Germany, Hungary, Bohemia, Naples, and Sicily. The empire also extends south and west to include possessions in North Africa and the Americas.

1520   King **Francis I** of France meets King **Henry VIII** of England at the Field of the Cloth of Gold in order to form an alliance against Holy Roman Emperor **Charles V.**

1520s   Swiss-born physician **Theophrastus Paracelsus** pioneers the use of chemicals to treat disease.

1521   **Martin Luther** is declared an "outlaw of the church" by **Charles V** at the Diet of Worms.

1521   The Ottoman Empire begins to reach its height when the sultan **Süleyman I** defeats Hungary in the Battle of Mohács.

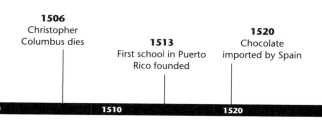

1506
Christopher
Columbus dies

1513
First school in Puerto
Rico founded

1520
Chocolate
imported by Spain

1500   1510   1520   1530

1525 **Francis I** is captured by the Spanish at the Battle of Pavia.

1527 King **Gustav I Vasa** begins establishing Lutheranism in Sweden.

1528 French diplomat **Baldassare Castiglione** publishes *Book of the Courtier.* The book is an immediate success and quickly becomes a guide to etiquette for both the bourgeoisie and the aristocracy in Europe.

1528 **Albrecht Dürer's** *The Four Books on Proportions* is published. It is his last and most important theoretical work.

1532 King **Henry VIII** is declared supreme head of the Church of England, completing the break between England and the Roman Catholic Church.

1534 French author **François Rabelais** begins publishing his most popular work, *Gargantua and Pantagruel.*

1535 **Thomas More** is beheaded after refusing to acknowledge the Act of Supremacy that makes King **Henry VIII** supreme head of the Church of England.

1536 French-born Protestant reformer **John Calvin** writes *Institutes of the Christian Religion,* which outlines his beliefs and gains him attention as an important religious leader.

1538 **Michelangelo Buonarroti** is commissioned to redesign the Capitoline Hill in Rome.

1540 Spanish priest **Ignatius of Loyola** founds the Society of Jesus (Jesuits). His Jesuit order eventually becomes the single most powerful weapon of the Catholic Reformation.

1543 *On the Revolution of Celestial Spheres* by Polish astronomer **Nicolaus Copernicus** is published. The

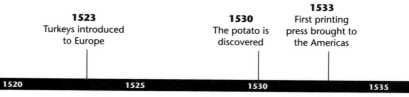

1523
Turkeys introduced
to Europe

1530
The potato is
discovered

1533
First printing
press brought to
the Americas

1520   1525   1530   1535

book gives important information about the orbits of the planets and begins a revolution in human thought by serving as the cornerstone of modern astronomy.

1543   Belgian anatomist **Andreas Vesalius** publishes *On the Fabric of the Human Body,* one of the most important contributions to human anatomy.

1544   **Gustav I Vasa** abolishes the elective monarchy and instills a hereditary monarchy.

1547   Emperor **Charles V** defeats German Protestant princes at the Battle of Mühlberg. Charles hopes his victory will stop the spread of Protestanism throughout the Holy Roman Empire.

1547   **Michelangelo Buonarroti** directs the construction of the new Saint Peter's Basilica.

1548   **Ignatius of Loyola** publishes *Spiritual Exercises.* This short but influential book outlines a thirty-day regimen, or systematic plan, of prayer and acts of self-denial and punishment, with the understanding that devotion to God must be central.

1550s   Italian architect **Andrea Palladio** popularizes the villa.

1550s   Italian composer **Giovanni Pierluigi da Palestrina** creates the oratorio, a lengthy religious choral work that features recitatives, arias, and choruses without action or scenery.

1555   **John Calvin** organizes an evangelical government in Geneva, Switzerland.

1555   Italian artist **Sofonisba Anguissola** paints *The Chess Game.* This painting is meant to demonstrate female excellence at an intellectual game.

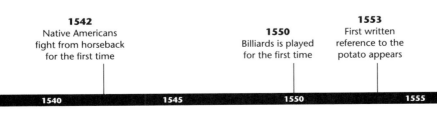

1542
Native Americans
fight from horseback
for the first time

1550
Billiards is played
for the first time

1553
First written
reference to the
potato appears

1540   1545   1550   1555

1555 French astrologer **Nostradamus** begins publishing *Centuries,* his best-selling book of predictions.

1556 Holy Roman Emperor **Charles V** abdicates the throne after building one of the largest empires in history.

1558 **Elizabeth I** begins her forty-five-year reign as queen of England and Ireland.

1560 **Catherine de Médicis** is named regent of France after the death of her husband King Henry II.

1560s **King Philip II** of Spain begins building the Escorial, an enormous complex of buildings north of Madrid.

1562 **Teresa de Ávila** founds the Reformed Discalced Carmelite Order.

1563 German artist **Pieter Bruegel** paints *Tower of Babel,* one of his most famous works.

1567 **Philip II** introduces the Spanish Inquisition in the Netherlands.

1570 **Andrea Palladio** publishes *Four Books on Architecture.*

1580 French author **Michel de Montaigne** publishes *Essays.* The work creates a new literary genre, the essay, in which he uses self-portrayal as a mirror of humanity in general.

1587 Queen **Elizabeth I** orders the execution of Mary, Queen of Scots after a conspiracy to assassinate Elizabeth is discovered.

1588 **Elizabeth I** reaches the height of her reign when her English naval fleet defeats the Spanish Armada.

1592 English playwright **William Shakespeare** begins his career in London and goes on to become one of the most famous playwrights in the world.

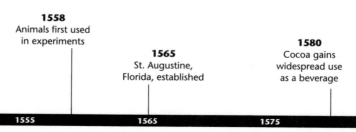

1558
Animals first used in experiments

1565
St. Augustine, Florida, established

1580
Cocoa gains widespread use as a beverage

1555 1565 1575 1585

1605 Spanish author **Miguel de Cervantes** publishes the first part of *Don Quixote,* one of the great masterpieces of world literature.

1606 Foremost English playwright **Ben Jonson**'s dramatic genius is fully revealed for the first time in *Volpone,* a satiric comedy that contains the playwright's harshest and most unrelenting criticism of human vice.

1609 Italian astronomer **Galileo Galilei** perfects the telescope and makes revolutionary observations of the universe.

1609 German astronomer **Johannes Kepler** publishes his first two laws of planetary motion in *New Astronomy.*

1611 King **James I** of England approves a new English translation of the Bible.

1616 The Roman Catholic Church orders **Galileo Galilei** to cease promoting the Sun-centered universe theory.

1616 Italian painter **Artemisia Gentileschi** becomes the first woman to be admitted to the Florentine Academy of Art.

1618 **Johannes Kepler** publishes his third law of planetary motion.

1620 English philosopher **Francis Bacon** publishes *New Method.*

1621 **James I** dissolves the British Parliament.

1624 German-born artist **Peter Paul Rubens** paints his famous *Self-portrait.*

1666 **Margaret Cavendish** publishes *The Description of a New World Called the Blazing World,* considered to be one of the first works of science fiction.

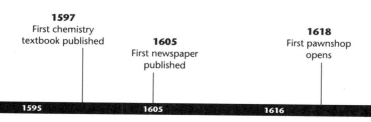

1597
First chemistry
textbook published

1605
First newspaper
published

1618
First pawnshop
opens

1595   1605   1616   1625

Words to Know

A

Abbey: A church connected with a monastery.

Abbot: A head of a monastery.

Abbess: A head of a convent.

Abdicate: To step down from the throne.

Absolution: Forgiveness of sins pronounced by a priest.

Absolutism: The concentration of all power in the hands of one ruler.

Adultery: Having sexual relations with someone who is not the person's husband or wife.

Agriculture: The growing of crops for food and other products.

Alchemy: The medieval science devoted to changing common metals into gold and silver.

Algebra: A form of arithmetic in which letters represent numbers.

Allegory: A story featuring characters with symbolic significance.

Altarpiece: A work of art that decorates an altar of a church.

Anatomy: The study of the structure of the body.

Annulment: An order that declares a marriage invalid.

Anti-Semitism: Prejudice against Jews.

Apprentice: One who learns a craft, trade, or profession from a master.

Aristocracy: The upper social class.

Armor: A protective suit made of iron worn by a soldier in battle.

Artillery: Various types of weapons.

Astrolabe: A device used to observe and calculate the distance of celestial bodies.

Astrology: The study of the heavens to predict future events.

Astronomy: The study of celestial bodies, such as planets, stars, the Sun, and the Moon.

Atheist: One who does not believe in God.

Augsburg Confession: An official statement of Lutheran churches prepared in 1530.

Auto da fé: Act of faith; public expression of commitment to Christianity required of supposed heretics during the Inquisition.

Autopsy: The dissection and examination of a corpse to determine the cause of death.

Axiom: A statement accepted as being true.

B

Babylonian Captivity: The name given to the period from 1307 to 1376 when the Roman Catholic pope lived in Avignon, France.

Baptism: A Christian ceremony in which a person is blessed with water and admitted to the Christian faith.

Barbarism: A lack of refinement or culture.

Baroque: The term used to describe the music, art, literature, and philosophy of the seventeenth century; exuberant, sensuous, expressive, and dynamic style.

Battle of Lepanto (1571): A sea battle in which the European Christian naval alliance defeated the fleet of the Ottoman Empire.

Battle of Mohács (1526): A conflict in which the Ottoman Empire conquered much of Hungary.

Battle of Mühlberg (1547): A conflict in which Holy Roman Emperor Charles V defeated the Schmalkaldic League.

Battle of Pavia: A conflict during the Italian Wars, in which Spain defeated France; it resulted in the Treaty of Madrid (1526), requiring France to give up claims to Italy, Burgundy, Flanders, and Artois.

Battle of Preveza (1538): A sea battle in which the Ottoman navy defeated the Genoan fleet and gained control of the eastern Mediterranean Sea.

Bewitch: To cast a spell over someone or something.

Bible: The Christian holy book.

Biology: The study of living organisms and their processes.

Bishop: The head of a church district.

Black Death: A severe epidemic of the bubonic plague that started in Europe and Asia in the fourteenth century.

Blasphemy: An expression of contempt toward God.

Bleeding: The procedure of draining blood from the body to cure disease.

Bourgeoisie: The middle class.

Brethren of the Common Life: The Protestant organization that founded humanist schools.

Bull: An order issued by a pope.

C

Cadaver: A dead body used for study purposes.

Canon: Church law or degree; clergyman at a cathedral.

Canonized: Named as a saint, or a person declared holy by the Roman Catholic Church.

Canton: A province or state.

Cardinal: A Roman Catholic Church official ranking directly below the pope.

Carnival: A celebration of a holy day.

Cartography: The study of maps and map-making.

Cartoon: A preparatory design or drawing for a fresco.

Castle: The residence of a lord and his knights, family, servants, and other attendants; eventually the center for a village and local government.

Catechism: A book of religious instructions in the form of questions and answers.

Cathedral: A large Christian house of worship.

Catholic Reformation: The reform movement within the Roman Catholic Church of the sixteenth and seventeenth centuries; also called the Counter Reformation.

Cavalry: Soldiers who ride horses in battle.

Censored: Suppressed or prohibited, as by the church.

Chamber music: Music composed for performance in a private room or small auditorium, usually with one performer for each part.

Chancellor: A chief secretary or administrator.

Chivalric code: A complex system of honor observed by knights during the Middle Ages.

Christ: The name for Jesus of Nazareth, founder of Christianity.

Christendom: The kingdom of Christ; name given to Europe by the Christian church.

Christianity: The religion founded by Jesus of Nazareth, who was also called the Christ.

City-state: A geographic region under the governmental control of a central city.

Classical period: The ancient Greek and Roman world, especially its literature, art, architecture, and philosophy.

Clergy: Church officials, including bishops, priests, and monks.

Cloister: Walkways with an arched open side supported by columns; also a term for an enclosed monastery or convent.

Coat of arms: An emblem signifying noble rank.

Commedia dell' arte: A type of comedy performed by professional acting companies that improvise plots depending on the materials at hand and the talents of the actors.

Commune: A district governed by a group of leaders called a corporation.

Communion: A Christian religious ceremony in which bread and wine represent the body and blood of Jesus of Nazareth (Christ).

Concordat of Bologna (1516): The agreement in which the Catholic Church in France came under direct control of the king.

Confession: An admission of sins to a priest; statement of belief forming the basis of a religious faith or denomination.

Confirmation: The act of conferring the gift of the Holy Spirit.

Confraternity: A society devoted to a charitable or religious cause.

Conscription: The requirement of all men above a certain age to serve in the military.

Constitution: A document that specifies the laws of a state and the rights of its citizens.

Consubstantiation: The concept that bread and wine in the Christian communion service are only symbolic of the body and blood of Christ, not transformed into the actual body and blood.

Convent: A house for women who are dedicated to religious life; also called a nunnery.

Conversion: The act of leaving one religion to accept another.

Converso: The Spanish word for a Jew who converted to Christianity.

Coup d'etat: A violent overthrow of a government.

Courtier: A member of a court; a gentleman.

Courtly love: Part of the chivalric code according to which a knight undertakes a quest (religious journey) or a tournament (game of combat) dedicated to a special lady.

Creed: A statement of religious beliefs.

Crucifix: A carved image of Christ crucified on a cross.

Crusades (1096–1291): A series of wars waged by Christians against Muslims in an effort to recapture the city of Jerusalem in the Holy Land; also wars against other non-Christians and Christians who challenged the church.

Curate: A clergyman in charge of a parish.

D

Democracy: A government based on the will of the majority of people.

Dialectic: Conversation based on discussion and reasoning.

Dialogue: A written work in which two or more speakers discuss a topic.

Diet: A meeting of representatives from states and districts in the Holy Roman Empire.

Diet of Augsburg (1530): A meeting in which Protestants and Catholics tried unsuccessfully to reach a compromise.

Diet of Nuremberg (1532): A meeting in which Protestant princes forced Emperor Charles V to continue toleration of Lutheranism indefinitely.

Diet of Speyer (1526): A meeting in which it was decided that each prince was responsible for settling religious issues in his own territory "until a general council of the whole Church could be summoned."

Diet at Speyer (1529): A meeting in which the 1526 Diet of Speyer decision was revoked; some Lutheran reformers protested, thus gaining the name "Protestants."

Diet of Worms (1521): A meeting in which Martin Luther refused to recant his beliefs and was declared an outlaw of the church by Emperor Charles V.

Diocese: A territorial district of a bishop.

Diplomat: A political negotiator or representative of a government.

Disciple: One who spreads the doctrines of a religious leader; one of the twelve followers of Jesus of Nazareth (Christ).

Disputation: A formal debate.

Divine right: The concept that a ruler is chosen directly by God.

Doctrine: Official church teachings.

Doge: The duke of Venice, Italy.

Dowry: Money, goods, or the estate that a woman brings to her husband in marriage.

Ducat: A gold coin used in various European countries.

Duel: A form of combat with weapons, usually pistols, between two persons in the presence of witnesses.

Dynasty: Rulers from the same family who hold political power for many generations.

E

East Roman Empire: In the Middle Ages, the countries of eastern Europe; based in Byzantium (now Istanbul, Turkey) and formed after the split of the Roman Empire in A.D. 395; also known as the Byzantine Empire.

East-West Schism (1052): The splitting of the Christian church into the Eastern Orthodox Church at Constantinople and the Roman Catholic Church in Rome.

Easter: The commemoration of Christ's resurrection, or rising from the dead.

Eclipse: The total or partial obscuring of one celestial body by another, as in the eclipse of the Sun by the Moon.

Edict of Worms: The statement issued by Emperor Charles V at the Diet of Worms in 1521; it condemned Lutheranism in all parts of the Holy Roman Empire.

The Elect: A few people chosen by God to receive salvation and to lead others who are not chosen for salvation.

Elector: A German prince entitled to vote for the Holy Roman Emperor.

Elegy: A poem expressing sorrow.

Epic: A literary work, usually a poem, in which the main character undertakes a long journey.

Epidemic: A widespread outbreak of disease.

Etiquette: Rules for proper manners.

Evangelism: A personal commitment to the teachings of Jesus of Nazareth (Christ).

Excommunicate: The act of being expelled from membership in a church.

Exile: Forcibly sending a person away from his or her native country or state.

F

Fable: A story with animal characters that teaches a moral lesson.

Facade: The outer front wall of a building.

Factions: Opposing sides in a conflict.

Faith: The acceptance of truth without question; also a profession of religious belief.

Farce: Literary or theatrical work based on exaggerated humor.

Fasting: Abstaining from food.

Feudalism: The social and political system of the Middle Ages, under which rulers granted land to lords in exchange for loyalty.

Fief: Territory granted to a nobleman by a king or emperor under feudalism.

First Helvetic Confession (1536): A statement of Protestant reform goals.

Florin: A coin made in Florence, Italy; later used by various European countries.

Free will: Exercise of individual choice independent of the will of God.

French Wars of Religion (1562–98): Series of conflicts between Catholics and Huguenots (Protestants) in France.

Fresco: A wall painting made by applying paint over a thin layer of damp lime plaster.

Friar: A man who belongs to a religious order that takes a vow of poverty.

G

Galaxy: A very large group of stars.

Galley: A ship propelled by oars.

Genre: A form of literature.

Geography: The study of the physical and cultural features of the Earth's surface.

Geometry: The branch of mathematics that deals with points, lines, angles, surfaces, and solids.

German Peasants' War (1524–26): Rebellion staged by peasants against Catholic princes in Germany.

Gospel: The word of God delivered by Jesus of Nazareth (Christ).

Grammar school: An elementary school; in the Renaissance, called Latin grammar school because students were required to learn Latin as the basis of the humanist curriculum.

Great Schism (1378–1418): The name given to a period of time when there were two Roman Catholic popes, one in Rome and one in Avignon, France.

Guild: An association of craftsmen, merchants, and professionals that trained apprentices and set standards of production or business operation.

H

Habit: The garment worn by a nun.

Hanseatic League: A trading network formed in the Middle Ages among cities around the Baltic Sea and the North Sea.

Heliocentric: Sun-centered.

Heresy: Violation of church laws.

Heretic: One who violates or opposes the teachings of the church.

Hermit: A member of a religious order who retires from society and lives in solitude.

Holy Roman Empire: A revival of the ancient Roman Empire; established by Otto the Great in A.D. 962.

Holy Spirit: The third person of the Christian Trinity (God the Father, the Son, and the Holy Spirit).

House: A family of rulers.

Huguenots: French Protestants.

Humanism: A human-centered literary and intellectual movement based on the revival of classical culture that started the Renaissance.

Humanistic studies: Five academic subjects consisting of grammar (rules for the use of a language), rhetoric (art of effective speaking and writing), moral philosophy (study of human conduct and values), poetry, and history.

Hundred Years' War (1337–1453): A series of intermittent conflicts between England and France over the French throne.

I

Idolatry: The worship of images, or false gods.

Incarnate: The spirit in bodily form.

Index of Prohibited Books: A list of books banned by the Roman Catholic Church.

Indulgence: The Roman Catholic Church practice of granting a partial pardon of sins in exchange for money.

Infantry: Soldiers trained to fight in the front line of battle.

Inquisition: An official court established by the Roman Catholic Church in 1233 for the purpose of hunting down and punishing heretics; during the Renaissance, it continued under the Spanish Inquisition (1492) and Roman Inquisition (1542).

Investiture struggle: An eleventh-century conflict between popes and rulers over the right to appoint bishops.

Islam: A religion founded by the prophet Muhammad.

Italian Wars (1494–1559): A conflict between France and Spain over control of Italy.

J

Janissaries: An elite army of the Ottoman Empire, composed of war captives and Christian youths forced into service.

Journeyman: The stage of apprenticeship during which one travels from job to job working in the shop of a master craftsman.

Joust: Combat on horseback between two knights with lances.

K

Kabbalah: Also cabala; system of Jewish religious and mystical thought.

Knight: A professional warrior who rode on horseback in combat; also known as a vassal, or one who pledged his loyalty to a lord and a king.

L

Laity: Unordained church members.

Lance: A long polelike weapon with a sharpened steel point.

Lent: The forty week days prior to Easter, the celebration of Christ's rising from the dead; a time devoted to prayer, penance, and reflection.

Limbo: A place where the unbaptized remain after death.

Linear perspective: A system derived from mathematics in which all elements of a composition are measured and arranged according to a single point (perspective).

Liturgy: Rites and texts used in a worship service.

Logarithms: A system of numbers with points that move on two lines of numbers, one point on increasing arithmetic value and the other moves on decreasing geometric values.

Loggia: An open, roofed porchlike structure with arches that overlooks a courtyard.

Logic: A system of thought based on reason.

Lord: One who was granted a large estate by a king in exchange for loyalty.

M

Madrigal: A song based on a poem or sacred text.

Magic: The use of spells or charms believed to have supernatural powers over natural forces; black magic is the use of evil spirits for destructive purposes; white magic is beneficial use of magic.

Magistrate: A government official similar to a judge; a mayor.

Marburg Colloquy (1529): Gathering of Protestant theologians who met to create a common creed (statement of beliefs) as a united front against Catholics.

Martyr: A person who voluntarily suffers death for a religious cause.

Masque: Court entertainment featuring masked actors, elaborate costumes, music, and dance.

Mass: The Roman Catholic worship service in which communion is taken.

Medical practitioner: An unlicensed healer who treats illness and disease.

Medieval: A term for the Middle Ages.

Mercenary: A hired soldier.

Mercury: A silver-colored, poisonous metallic element.

Metallurgy: The study and use of metals.

Metaphysics: The study of the nature of reality and existence.

Meteorology: The science that deals with the study of weather patterns.

Middle Ages: A period in European history that began after the downfall of the West Roman Empire in the fourth and fifth centuries and continued into the fifteenth century; once called the Dark Ages.

Midwife: One who assists in childbirth.

Mistress: A woman who has a continuing sexual relationship with a married man and is not his wife.

Monarchs: Kings and queens who have sole ruling power.

Monastery: A house for monks, members of a religious order.

Monk: A man who is a member of a religious order and lives in a monastery.

Monopoly: Exclusive control or possession of a trade or business.

Moors: Muslim Arab and Berber conquerors of Spain.

Morisco: The Spanish word for a Muslim who converted to Christianity.

Mortal sin: An act of wrongdoing that causes spiritual death.

Mosque: A Muslim house of worship.

Muslim: A follower of the Islamic religion.

Mysticism: Religion based on intense spiritual experiences.

N

Natural history: An ancient and medieval term for the study of nature.

New Testament: The second part of the Bible, the Christian holy book.

New World: The European term for the Americas.

Nobility: Members of the upper social class.

Novella: A form of short fictitious story originating in Italy.

Nun: A woman who is a member of a religious order and lives in a convent.

O

Occult: An aspect of religion that relies on magic and mythology.

Old Testament: The first part of the Bible, the Christian holy book.

Opera: A musical work that combines choruses in complex harmony, solo ensembles, arias, dances, and independent instrumental pieces.

Oratorio: A lengthy religious choral work that features singing that resembles speaking in the form of arias and choruses without action or scenery.

Oratory: Public speaking.

Orbit: The path of a heavenly body such as a planet.

P

Pagan: A person who has no religious beliefs or worships more than one god.

Papacy: The office of the pope.

Papal: Relating to a pope or the Roman Catholic Church.

Papal State: The territory owned by the Roman Catholic Church and governed by the pope.

Parish: A local church community.

Parliament: The main governing body of Britain.

Patron: A financial supporter.

Peace of Westphalia (1648): An agreement that ended the Thirty Years' War; by it, Catholic and Protestant states were given equal status within the Holy Roman Empire.

Penance: An act performed to seek forgiveness of sins.

Persecution: Harassment for religious beliefs.

Philosophy: The search for a general understanding of values and reality through speculative thinking.

Physics: The science that deals with energy and matter and their interactions.

Piety: Dutifulness in religion.

Pilgrimage: A religious journey.

Plague: A widespread communicable disease.

Planetary motion: The movement of planets around the Sun.

Pope: The supreme head of the Roman Catholic Church.

Predestination: The belief that the fate of all humans is determined by a divine force.

Prince: A political and military leader; Renaissance ruler.

Prior: The head of a monastery.

Protestantism: Christian religion established by reformers who separated from the Roman Catholic Church.

Protestant Reformation: The reform movement that established a Christian religion separate from the Roman Catholic Church.

Purgatory: A place between heaven and hell.

Q

Quadrant: A device in the shape of a quarter circle that measures angles up to 90 degrees and is used for determining altitudes.

Quest: A religious journey.

R

Regent: One who rules in place of a minor or an absent monarch.

Relief: A carving or sculpture with detail raised above the surface.

Renaissance: The transition period in European history from medieval to modern times, marked by a revival of classical culture, which brought innovations in the arts and literature and initiated modern science.

Rhetoric: Art of effective speaking and writing.

Roman Catholic Church: Christian religion based in Rome, Italy, and headed by a pope.

S

Sack of Rome (1527): Destruction of parts of Rome by armies of Emperor Charles V.

Sacraments: Rites of the Catholic Church: communion, baptism, confirmation, penance, anointing of the sick, marriage, and holy offices.

Sacrilege: The violation of anything considered sacred to God.

Saint: A person who is declared holy by the Catholic Church.

Salic law: A law stating that a male could be the only legitimate heir to the throne.

Salon: A gathering of nobles for discussion of literature and ideas.

Salvation: The forgiveness of sins.

Satire: Criticism through the use of humor.

Schmalkaldic League: A military alliance of German Protestant princes formed in 1531.

Scholasticism: Medieval scholarly method that combined Christian teachings with Greek philosophy.

Scriptures: The text of the Bible, the Christian holy book.

Sect: A small religious group.

Secular: Nonreligious; worldly.

Seignor: An owner of a large estate; also called a lord.

Seignorialism: European social system inherited from the Roman practice of forcing poor people to be dependent on a large landowner called a seignor or lord.

Serf: A peasant who was loyal to a lord and worked on land under the system of feudalism.

Sextant: An instrument used for measuring angular distances.

Simony: The selling of offices in the Roman Catholic Church.

Smallpox: A contagious disease caused by a virus that produces severe skin sores.

Soul: Eternal spirit.

Spanish Armada: The fleet of heavily armored ships built by Spain to defeat England.

Sultan: Arabian king.

Swiss Brethren: A Protestant group who believe in adult baptism; also called Anabaptists.

Swiss Confederation: An alliance of cantons (states) in Switzerland.

Synagogue: Jewish house of worship.

T

Tapestry: A large embroidered wall hanging.

Telescope: A tube-shaped instrument with a lens or mirror used for viewing distant objects.

Theologian: A scholar who studies and teaches religion.

Thirty Years' War (1618–48): A social, religious, and political conflict involving all major world powers; known as the first "world war."

Tithe: Contribution of one-tenth of a church member's income to the church.

Topography: The study of natural and man-made features of a place.

Tournament: A game in which knights engaged in combat with lances on horseback.

Tragedy: A drama that portrays the rise and fall of an honorable man.

Transubstantiation: The belief that bread and wine actually become the body and blood of Christ.

Treatise: A written study of a topic or issue.

Treaty of Cateau-Cambrésis (1559): The peace agreement between France and Spain that ended the Italian Wars, giving Spain control of Italy.

Trigonometry: The branch of mathematics dealing with the study of triangles.

Triptych: A three-panel artwork.

Troubadours: French and Italian poet-musicians.

U

Universe: The totality of the world, including the Earth and the heavens.

V

Vassal: A knight; nobleman soldier who pledged loyalty to a lord.

Vatican: The palace of the pope.

Vestimentary laws: Laws relating to the clothes, or vestments, worn by clergymen.

Villa: A country house; a popular architectural style during the Renaissance.

Vulgate: The official Latin version of the Bible.

W

War of the Roses (1455–85): Conflict between the houses of York and Lancaster in England that resulted in the founding of the House of Tudor.

West Roman Empire: Countries of western Europe; based in Rome, Italy, and formed after the split of the Roman Empire in A.D. 395.

Witchcraft: The practice of communicating with supernatural spirits to bring about certain events or results.

Y

Year of Jubilee: A special spiritual celebration held every twenty-five years by the Catholic Church.

Leonardo da Vinci

April 15, 1452
Vinci, Italy
May 2, 1519
Amboise, France

Painter, scientist

One of the greatest figures of the Renaissance was the painter Leonardo da Vinci. Known as Leonardo, he was considered the ideal "Renaissance man," an individual whose talents spanned a variety of subjects. He was an innovator in the fields of both art and science, uniquely combining these two activities as he investigated the world around him. Although he completed relatively few paintings, he played a crucial role in creating and shaping the art of the High Renaissance (1495–1520), the period when Renaissance culture reached its height in Italy. He was also interested in architecture, sculpture, and urban planning, though he is not known to have done work in these areas. Leonardo had an enormous influence on other artists, and his achievements were admired by such great Renaissance painters as **Michelangelo** (1475–1564; see entry) and **Raphael** (1483–1520; see entry).

Perfects his own style

Leonardo was born on April 15, 1452, near the village of Vinci about twenty-five miles west of Florence. He was the

"As a well-spent day brings happy sleep, so life well used brings happy death."

Leonardo da Vinci in The Notebooks *quoted on* The Quotations Page. *[Online] Available http://www. quotationspage.com/quotes. php3?author=Leonardo+da+ Vinci, April 5, 2002.*

Leonardo da Vinci.
Photograph courtesy of The Library of Congress.

illegitimate (born out of wedlock) son of Piero da Vinci, a prominent notary (one who records legal documents) of Florence, and Caterina, a peasant girl. Piero had no other children until much later and he raised his son himself, a common practice at the time. He arranged for Caterina to marry a local villager. In 1467, at age fifteen, Leonardo was apprenticed (sent to learn a craft, trade, or profession) to Andrea del Verrocchio (1435–1488), the leading artist in Florence, which was then the center of the Renaissance. Verrocchio was a sculptor, painter, and goldsmith noted for his craftsmanship. Leonardo stayed on as an assistant in Verrocchio's shop after completing his apprenticeship. His earliest known painting is a product of his collaboration (working together) with the master. In 1472 Leonardo joined the Compagnia di San Luca, or painters guild, in Florence. (A guild was a professional organization that supervised the training of craftsmen.)

In Verrocchio's *Baptism of Christ* (c. 1475), Leonardo executed one of the two angels as well as the distant landscape. He also added the final touches to the figure of Jesus Christ (name for Jesus of Nazareth, founder of Christianity), determining the texture of the flesh. Collaboration on a major project by a master artist and his assistant was standard procedure in the Italian Renaissance. Leonardo's work was special, however, because he did not follow the usual approach and produce a slightly less skilled version of Verrocchio's style. Instead, he perfected an original technique that altered his teacher's method. For instance, Leonardo suggested a new flexibility within the figures in *Baptism of Christ*. He accomplished this by changing hard metallic effects to soft yielding ones and increasing the slight changes in light and shade.

Around 1478 Leonardo set up his own studio. Three years later he received a church commission for an altarpiece (a work of art that decorates the space above an altar, a table used as the center of a worship service), the *Adoration of the Magi*. This unfinished painting depicts the story of the three Magi (kings), also known as the Wise Men of the East, told in the book of Matthew in the Bible (the Christian holy book). The Magi traveled to Bethlehem from the East (ancient Persia; present-day Iran) to pay homage to the newborn Jesus. The Adoration of the Magi had been a popular subject in art since the Middle Ages (a period lasting from around 400 to 1400). In his painting Leonardo showed a new approach with the

Masaccio: Father of Renaissance Painting

The Florentine painter Masaccio (pronounced mah-ZAHT-choh; Tommaso di Giovanni di Simone Guidi; 1401–1428) is considered the father of Renaissance painting. He was the first painter to utilize linear perspective (also known as one-point perspective). Invented by the Florentine architect Filippo Brunelleschi, linear perspective is a system derived from mathematics in which all elements of a composition are measured and arranged from a single point of view, or perspective. Masaccio was Brunelleschi's friend and may have learned linear perspective from him. Masaccio used the technique to achieve the effect of light coming from one direction and illuminating figures. Through the interplay of light and shadow, these figures seem to have three dimensions and exist in actual space. An equally important feature of this technique is that it gives the viewer a sense of looking at a scene along with the painter.

Masaccio's most celebrated work, dated 1425 to 1427, is a series of frescoes in the Brancacci Chapel in the Church of Santa Maria del Camine in Florence. (A fresco is a wall painting that is made by first spreading moist lime plaster on the wall and then applying paint. Early Renaissance painters used tempera, a water-based paint made with egg yolks and color pigments, that is, substances containing color derived from plant or animal matter.) One scene, *Expulsion from Paradise,* depicts Adam and Eve as they are cast out of the Garden of Eden. The painting vividly portrays their profound remorse and anguish through their body language and facial expressions. Masaccio achieved this sense of human drama in all of his works. Although he only lived until the age of twenty-seven, he had a profound impact on the art world. Every major artist of the fifteenth and sixteenth centuries in Florence started his career by studying Masaccio's murals.

depiction of human drama through a sense of continuing movement. A crowd of spectators, with odd and varied faces, flutters around and peers at Mary (mother of Jesus), who is holding the baby Jesus. In the background the three Magi are mounted on horses that prance among intricate architectural ruins. The painting also illustrates a strong sense of order. Traditionally, in paintings of this story Mary and Jesus appeared at one side of the picture and the Magi approached from the other side. Leonardo departed from tradition by placing Mary and Jesus in the center of the composition. He also used linear perspective to depict the ruins in the background. Also known as one-point perspective, linear perspective was invented by the Florentine architect Filippo Brunelleschi (pronounced broo-nail-LAYS-kee;1377–1446). It is a system derived from mathematics in which all elements of a composition are measured and arranged from a single point of view, or perspective. The Florentine artist Masaccio, known as the father of Renaissance painting, was the first to use linear perspective extensively (see accompanying box).

Moves to Milan

Leonardo left Florence in 1482 to accept the post of court artist to Ludovico Sforza (1452–1508), duke of Milan. His first Milanese painting was the altarpiece *Virgin of the Rocks*. Although the *Virgin of the Rocks* was highly original, Leonardo used the medieval tradition of showing Mary and Jesus in a cave. This gave him the opportunity to experiment with dimmed light, which is coming from two sources, one behind the cave and the other in front of it. (Leonardo once commented that an artist should practice drawing at dusk and in courtyards with walls painted black.) The technique highlights the four figures—Mary and Jesus and another woman and infant—in a soft, shadowy atmosphere. The distinctive feature of the painting is the pyramidal (pyramid shaped) grouping of the figures, which unifies the composition and focuses the eye of the viewer on the central scene.

The other surviving painting of Leonardo's years in Milan is the *Last Supper* (1497). It was commissioned by the duke for a wall in the refectory (dining hall) of the convent (a house for women who are dedicated to religious life) of Santa Maria delle Grazie. For this painting Leonardo decided not to use fresco, which makes areas of color appear distinct and does not allow for shading. Instead, he experimented with oil-based paint, which is more easily blended, but his efforts were unsuccessful. The paint did not adhere well to the wall, and within fifty years the scene was reduced to a confused series of spots. When the government of Milan was overthrown by the French invasion in 1499, Leonardo left Milan and returned to Florence.

Recognized as great painter

Leonardo was received as a great man in Florence. During his years in the city (1500–06), he completed more projects

Leonardo's *Mona Lisa* became one of the most famous portraits in the Western world. *Reproduced by permission of the New York Public Library Picture Collection.*

than in any other period of his life. In 1503 he was invited to paint a large-scale fresco that celebrated the Battle of Anghiara, in which Florence defeated Milan in 1440. The fresco was to be painted on the walls of the newly built Council Chamber of the Republic in the Palazzo della Signoria. For the *Battle of Anghiara* Leonardo experimented with an oil-based paint on a primed (prepared with a sealing substance) wall surface. This process proved to be ineffective because the paint did not dry.

The central section of the composition, which was destroyed during a restoration project in 1565, is now known through numerous copies made in the sixteenth and seventeenth centuries. As indicated in a copy made by the Flemish painter **Peter Paul Rubens** (1577–1640; see entry) in 1615, Leonardo depicted the extreme physical exertion of men and horses engaged in furious battle. The group of central figures displays faces distorted by rage or pain. Even the heads of the horses, with flaring nostrils and gnashing teeth, were treated in this expressive manner. Shortly after Leonardo began the *Battle of Anghiara* his younger rival, Michelangelo, was commissioned to paint *Battle of Cascina,* another celebrated Florentine victory, for the same room in the Palazzo della Signoria.

In 1503, while working on the *Battle of Anghiara* Leonardo started painting the *Mona Lisa.* It is a portrait of Lisa di Anton Giocondo, the young wife of the prominent Florentine citizen Francesco del Giocondo. The *Mona Lisa* became one of the most famous portraits in the Western world because of Lisa's mysterious smile, which is in the process of either appearing or disappearing. Leonardo had abandoned the *Anghiara* project by 1508, when he was called back to Milan by Charles d'Amboise, the French governor. Leonardo worked on an equestrian (rider mounted on a horse) statue, but he produced no new paintings. Instead he turned more and more to scientific observation (see accompanying box). In 1513 the French were temporarily driven out of Milan and Leonardo moved to Rome. He received no other commissions, however, and at the end of 1516 he left Italy forever. He spent the last three years of his life at Amboise, France, in the small residence of Cloux (later called Clos-Lucé), near the summer palace of the king of France, **Francis I** (1494–1547; see entry). Given the title of *Premier peintre, architecte et méchanicien du Roi* (first painter, architect, and mechanic of the King), Leonardo lived as an honored guest of Francis I. Leonardo did no other major work, and he spent his time on his notebooks, in which he wrote about science and art theory (general ideas and criteria concerning the making of artworks).

Pursues interest in science

For Leonardo art theory was closely related to scientific investigation. Throughout most of his life he was immersed

Leonardo's Submarine

Leonardo designed many mechanical devises, including a submarine. He refused to share his ideas for this underwater mode of transportation—except to say that it involved a tube and wine skins or pieces of cork—because he feared it would be used for destructive purposes. Here is what Leonardo wrote about his submarine in his notebook:

How by an appliance many are able to remain for some time under water. How and why I do not describe my method of remaining under water for as long a time as I can remain without food; and this I do not publish or divulge on account of the evil nature of men who would practise assassinations at the bottom of the seas by breaking the ships in their lowest parts and sinking them together with the crews who are in them; although I will furnish particulars of others which are not dangerous, for above the surface of the water emerges the mouth of a tube by which they draw breath, supported upon wine skins or pieces of cork.

Source: Selections from the Notebooks of Leonardo da Vinci. *Irma A. Richter, editor. New York: Oxford University Press, 1977, pp. 96–97.*

in the study of science. He was especially interested in studying anatomy (structure of the body) in order to understand the human form. In fact, he dissected cadavers (human corpses) so he could examine the function of muscles and to determine how the vocal cords produce sound. From the 1490s until 1515 Leonardo made extensive notes on his observations, including analytical drawings for illustrations in a treatise on anatomy, which he never completed.

Leonardo also worked on several inventions. He designed many mechanical devises, such as a screw jack, a two-wheeled hoist, an "armored car," a gun with three racks of barrels, and even a submarine. He refused to share his ideas for a submarine, however, because he feared it would be used for destructive purposes. Leonardo's best-known invention was a flying machine, which he designed by observing birds in flight and the motions of air. He also mastered mathematics. For instance, he applied geometry and proportion to create a new sense of order in his drawings and paintings. He translated his study of optics and many of his theories of vision into mathematical terms. Leonardo used his knowledge of physical geography to investigate the origin of fossils and the utilization of water power.

Leonardo died at Cloux and was buried in the palace church of Saint-Florentin. But the church was devastated during the French Revolution (1789–99) and completely torn down at the beginning of the nineteenth century. Hence, his grave can no longer be located. Leonardo's assistant, Francesco Melzi, inherited his estate.

Influences other artists

Leonardo had considerable influence on artists of his own day and later times. Some of his views on art, which had been circulating since the sixteenth century, were published in 1651 in *Trattato della pittura* (Treatise on painting). This is a collection of his writings taken from numerous manuscripts. The small number of Leonardo's surviving paintings show his achievements as an artist. He made contributions to every artistic form, from portraits to religious narratives. He gave new insights into figure grouping, space, individual characterization, and light and shade. Many of his works inspired copies, especially by Milanese artists such as Andrea Solari (after 1495–1514) and Bernardo Luini (died 1532). In Florence his compositions were carefully studied by Raphael. Leonardo's *Battle of Anghiari* and Michelangelo's design for *Battle of Cascina*, were the "school for the world," in the words of Italian sculptor Benvenuto Cellini (1500–1571). Even in the nineteenth century, long after the *Battle of Anghiari* had disappeared, aspects of its design continued to intrigue artists throughout Europe.

For More Information

Books

Gelb, Michael. *How to Think Like Leonardo Da Vinci: Seven Steps to Genius Every Day.* New York: Delacorte Press, 1998.

Lafferty, Peter. *Leonardo da Vinci.* New York: Bookwright, 1990.

Nuland, Sheriwn B. *Leonardo da Vinci.* New York: Viking, 2000.

Video Recordings

Masterpieces of Italian Art. Volume: Da Vinci, Michelangelo, Raphael and Titian. New York: VPI-AC Video Inc., 1990.

Web Sites

"da Vinci, Leonardo." *Artcyclopedia.* [Online] Available http://artcyclopedia. com/artists/leonardo_da_vinci.html, April 5, 2002.

"da Vinci, Leonardo." *National Museum of Science and Technology.* [Online] Available http://www.museoscienza.org/english/leonardo/leonardo.html, April 5, 2002.

"da, Vinci, Leonard." *The Quotations Page.* [Online] Available http://www.quotationspage.com/quotes.php3?author=Leonardo+da+Vinci, April 5, 2002.

"da Vinci, Leonardo." *WebMuseum.* [Online] Available http://mexplaza.udg.mx/wm/paint/auth/vinci/, April 5, 2002.

"Leonardo da Vinci." *MSN Encarta.* [Online] Available http://encarta.msn.com/find/Concise.asp?z=1&pg=2&ti=761561520, April 5, 2002.

Martin Luther

November 10, 1483
Eisleben, Germany
February 18, 1546
Eiselben, Germany

Scholar, professor, writer, religious reformer

"I began to understand." he wrote later, "that the righteousness of God is that gift of God by which a righteous [morally upright] man lives, namely, faith, and that ... the merciful God justifies us by faith..."

Martin Luther.

Martin Luther. *Reproduced by permission of the National Museum of Stockholm.*

The fifteenth and sixteenth centuries were a time of transition from the Middle Ages (c. 400 –1400; also called the medieval period) to the modern era. Throughout the Middle Ages the Roman Catholic Church (a Christian religion headed by a pope and based in Rome, Italy) controlled all aspects of social, political, and religious life. It was the largest institution (complex organization) in western Europe and consisted of an elaborate hierarchy (ranks of officials)—the pope, cardinals (officials ranking below the pope), bishops (heads of church districts), canons (legal administrators), priests (heads of local churches), and numerous other clergymen. The pope was considered infallible (always correct), and he was the most powerful ruler in Europe. The Catholic Church was also immensely wealthy, owning vast properties and collecting huge sums in taxes, tithes (one-tenth of income), and other forms of payment from the people.

Beginning in the fifteenth century, the medieval view of the world underwent radical change. Renaissance humanists (scholars who revived the literary culture of ancient Greece and Rome) had freed scholarship and the arts from the sponsorship of the church. In so doing, humanists not only rediscovered the individual but also challenged the blind acceptance of authority and encouraged the individual search for truth through reason. Now people were seeking a better way to understand God in terms of their own experience. Into this changing world was born Martin Luther. Now known as the father of the Protestant Reformation, Luther was a German priest who singlehandedly altered the course of European history.

"Save me, Saint Anne"

Martin Luther was born at Eisleben in Saxony (a duchy in northwest Germany) on November 10, 1483, the son of Hans and Margaret Luther. His parents were of peasant stock, but his father had worked hard to raise the family's social status. Hans Luther began his career as a miner, then became the owner of several small mines that brought the family a fair degree of financial comfort. This process took nearly a decade, however, and life for the nine Luther children (five boys and four girls) was sometimes difficult. Young Martin was severely beaten by both his mother and his father for relatively minor offenses. This type of discipline was common at the time. In 1490 Martin was sent to the Latin school at Mansfeld, Germany. Seven years later he was sent to a better school in Magdeburg, Germany. In 1498, after he had shown academic excellence, he enrolled in a school located in Eisenach, Germany. Here he met Johann Braun, a dedicated cleric who became his role model.

Luther's early education was typical of late-fifteenth-century practices. To a young man in his circumstances, only the law and the church offered likely avenues to success. His parents believed that the financial success of their children would guarantee them, the elder Luthers, comfort in their old age. Hans Luther had a dislike for the priesthood, a feeling that probably influenced his decision that Martin should be a lawyer. In 1501 Martin enrolled at the University of Erfurt, one of the oldest and most prestigious universities in Germany. Within four years he earned both bachelor's and master's degrees. In 1505 he had just begun the study of law and was on his way to a career in service to the church or to one of the many German princes (rulers of states). Then he abruptly abandoned the university for the disciplined life of a monastery (house for men in a religious order). This dramatic change occurred on July 2, 1505, while Luther was returning to the university from a visit with his parents. Along the way he was suddenly caught in a thunderstorm. As lightning struck nearby, he cried out in terror to his patron saint: "Save me, Saint Anne, and I will become a monk." Just two weeks later, Luther joined the Eremites of Saint Augustine (a religious order) in Erfurt. He was ordained a priest within a year.

Luther was no ordinary monk, for he was deeply troubled by the teachings of the church. Since the early Middle Ages, Catholic leaders had taught that the church was the only link between the individual and God. The church provided salvation (deliverance from sin, or wrongdoing) to repentant sinners through the sacraments (holy rituals), most notably communion (also called the Holy Eucharist). Administered in a ceremony called the mass, communion is a ritual in which bread and wine symbolize the body and blood of Jesus of Nazareth (called Christ), the founder of Christianity. Also, the church taught that the individual had a duty to use his or her own free will (ability to make independent choices) to love and serve God. This was the way to earn salvation from God. In short, the individual participated in his or her own salvation through good deeds. Such teachings brought comfort to many, but they caused distress for Luther. His problem was that no matter how hard he "worked" at earning his salvation, he could not find any peace with God.

Luther found the answer to his spiritual problem sometime during the fall of 1515. By then he was a professor of theology (study of religion) at the University of Wittenberg and in charge eleven monasteries. The answer came while he was preparing a series of lectures in his study in a tower of the monastery. He was pondering the meaning of verse 17 in chapter 1 of the book of Romans in the New Testament (second part of the Bible, the Christian holy book): "For it is the righteousness of God revealed from faith to faith; as it is written, The just shall live by faith." In that little verse was contained the heart of Luther's problem, as well as the solution. He was perplexed by the two phrases, "the righteousness of God" and " The just shall live by faith." In accordance with church teachings, Luther understood "the righteousness of God" to mean that a righteous, even angry, God punishes all

Indulgences

Indulgences began as gifts of money given to the clergy in appreciation or gratitude for forgiveness of sins (wrongdoing). Soon, however, indulgences began to represent an outward showing of grief for sins. People would pay for indulgences to prove to the church and others that they were truly repentant for their sins. In the thirteenth century, the Catholic Church formulated what was called the "treasury of merits." It was a spiritual bank of sorts that "contained" the good works performed by Jesus Christ, the saints, and all pious, or devoted, Christians. In other words, because Jesus and the saints had lived better lives than necessary to get into heaven, their good deeds had been left on Earth in the treasury of merits. Good deeds from this treasury could be redistributed to Christian believers in the form of indulgences. One would give money to his or her clergyman, who would in turn make a "withdrawal" from the spiritual bank on behalf of person who paid for the indulgence. This system was supposed to reduce the amount of time the soul (spirit of a dead person) spent in purgatory (place between heaven and hell), but many church members did not fully understand this aspect of indulgences. It was widely believed that people could sin as much as possible and still buy their way into heaven by purchasing indulgences.

sinners. Such a view caused him to hate the God he knew he should love. Then, as Luther meditated over the verse, he realized that a morally upright person gains salvation through faith in God alone, and not through the interpretations of the Scriptures that were enforced by church officials. Luther's idea came to be known as justification of faith.

Makes revolutionary discovery

Luther had made a revolutionary discovery—that salvation comes through faith alone. He then reached an even more startling conclusion. This truth is revealed in the Bible, not through the mass and other sacraments (holy rites) administered by priests. Therefore, all of the clergy, from the pope down to the parish priest, were unnecessary. Luther did not immediately challenge the church with this discovery. What spurred him to action was the appearance, in 1517, of a monk peddling indulgences (payments to church officials for

Luther's "Ninety-Five Theses"

Martin Luther wrote down his theological disagreements with the Catholic Church in the "Ninety-Five Theses." His intention was to generate a discussion that could help the church eliminate corruption. Luther was not planning to leave the church or cause the controversy that eventually resulted in the Protestant Reformation.

The following is only a brief excerpt of the entire list of Luther's theses, but it gives the reader a sense of the issues. Notice that Luther spoke of an individual relationship with God, and he dismissed the idea of purgatory. He emphasized that personal penance (showing sorrow for sin) and faith are the only way to gain salvation from sin. The roles of the pope and priests were greatly reduced by Luther. For instance, he argued that the pope could not remit (grant forgiveness for) sins because the act of penance (an act performed to seek forgiveness of sins) should take place only between the individual and God. In fact, Luther called into question the authority of the church to create canons (laws) and administer sacraments, because such authority rests only in God, not the church.

1. When our Lord and Master Jesus Christ said, "Repent" [Matt. 4:17], he willed the entire life of believers to be one of repentance.

2. This word cannot be understood as referring to the sacrament of penance, that is, confession and satisfaction, as administered by the clergy.

forgiveness of sins; see accompanying box) outside Wittenberg. The monk was selling indulgences on behalf of the new archbishop of Mainz, twenty-three-year-old Albert von Hohenzollern, who had "purchased" his position. To pay back the funds he borrowed from the Fugger bank in Augsburg to finance the purchase, Albert was authorized by Pope Leo X (1475–1521; reigned 1513–21) to sell indulgences in Germany.

The abuse of the indulgence system was evident in the aggressive sales tactics of John Tetzel (1465–1519), an experienced indulgence salesman who appeared outside Luther's door in October 1517. Tetzel was selling indulgences to finance the new Saint Peter's Basilica, which was under construction in Rome. He claimed that indulgences could be purchased for relatives already dead, or for sins one might commit in the future. "As soon as the coin in the coffer rings," Tetzel said, "the soul from purgatory springs."

3. Yet it does not mean solely inner repentance; such inner repentance is worthless unless it produces various outward mortifications [humiliations] of the flesh.

4. The penalty of sin remains as long as the hatred of self, that is, true inner repentance, until our entrance into the kingdom of heaven.

5. The pope neither desires nor is able to remit any penalties except those imposed by his own authority or that of the canons.

6. The pope cannot remit any guilt, except by declaring and showing that it has been remitted by God; or, to be sure, by remitting guilt in cases reserved to his judgment. If his right to grant remission in these cases were disregarded, the guilt would certainly remain unforgiven.

7. God remits guilt to no one unless at the same time he humbles him in all things and makes him submissive to his vicar, the priest.

8. The penitential canons are imposed only on the living, and, according to the canons themselves, nothing should be imposed on the dying.

9. Therefore the Holy Spirit through the pope is kind to us insofar as the pope in his decrees always makes exception of the article of death and of necessity.

10. Those priests act ignorantly and wickedly who, in the case of the dying, reserve canonical penalties for purgatory.

Source: Noll, Mark A. Confessions and Catechisms of the Reformation. *Vancouver, B.C.: Regent College Publishing, 1997, pp. 29–30.*

Posts theses at Wittenberg

Luther felt impelled to respond to the obvious misuse of indulgences. According to popular legend, on October 31, 1517 (the eve of All Saints' Day; now called Halloween), Luther defiantly nailed a document titled "Ninety-Five Theses or Disputation on the Power and Efficacy of Indulgences" to the door of the church at the University of Wittenberg. Some scholars downplay the drama of this act, suggesting that Luther simply tacked the "Ninety-Five Theses" to the church door, which served as a kind of bulletin board at the university. Others say he attached the theses to the letter he wrote to the archbishop of Mainz, protesting the sale of indulgences. In any case, he intended the document as an invitation to his colleagues to debate the issue.

Most modern scholars agree that Luther never intended to begin a widespread reform movement within the

Catholic Church. He merely wanted to spark academic debate about a serious issue. Initially, his protest fell on deaf ears, since the archbishop of Mainz was sharing the profits of indulgence sales with the pope. Had someone not translated the "Ninety-Five Theses" from Latin (the language used in all formal communications) into German, they might have gone unnoticed. With the aid of the recently invented printing press, the translation appeared throughout Germany. The theses were thus made available to theologians, scholars, and anyone else who could read German.

Called before Diet of Worms

Although Luther had directly challenged the authority of the pope, Leo X did not move immediately to silence him. In 1519 Luther attended a debate at the University of Leipzig. The debate raged on for eighteen days before it was called off. Luther had defended his beliefs by stating that people should live their lives by following the Bible, not the pope. He said people could find their own salvation through faith—they did not need the church. Luther began writing his views in pamphlets, and his ideas soon spread throughout Germany. Many people backed him. In June 1520 Leo X issued a bull (papal order) criticizing Luther and excommunicating (expelling) him from the church. When Luther received this document, he publicly burned it. The following April, Luther was summoned to the town of Worms, where an assembly of German princes (called the Diet) had been convened by the new Holy Roman Emperor, nineteen-year-old **Charles V** (1500–1558; ruled 1519–56; see entry). The Diet wanted Luther to withdraw his views. He refused, so Charles declared him an outlaw of the church and ordered his arrest. But Frederick the Wise (1463–1525), Luther's friend and the prince who ruled Wittenberg, kidnapped Luther and hid him in Wartburg Castle, one of Frederick's residences near Eisenach. There, over the next eleven months, Luther spent his time translating the New Testament from Latin into German.

Returning to Wittenberg in March 1522, Luther tried to unify his followers. By then, almost half the people of Germany had adopted his views. Many called themselves "Lutherans" (only later did the reformers come to be known as Protestants). Yet the movement began to fragment almost immediately. The Bible may be the final authority, but according to Luther every believer is his own priest, his own interpreter of what the Bible says. As a result of Luther's view, numerous Protestant sects (groups) were formed—and they are still being formed. In 1525 Luther married Katherine von Bora (1499–1552), a former nun (a woman who belongs to a religious order). They had six children, some of whom died early, and adopted eleven others. By all accounts, their home was a happy one. Luther called his wife "my beloved Katie," and she was a great source of strength for him.

Protestants fall into disunity

All that happened after the Diet of Worms was anticlimactic. Luther tried to halt the extreme views of some of his followers. But fragmentation, not unity, was to characterize the future of the Protestant churches. In 1530 Philipp Melanchthon (1497–1560), Luther's closest associate, drafted a confession (statement) of faith. Both he and Luther hoped it might provide a basis for unity between the Lutherans and the Roman Catholic Church. Rejected by the Diet of Augsburg, Melanchthon's confession, called the "Augsburg Confession," became the basis for the doctrine (beliefs and teachings) of Lutheran churches. Luther introduced numerous reforms in the worship service. He placed an emphasis on preaching and teaching from the Bible, and he reintroduced music and congregational singing. A fine musician, Luther wrote many popular hymns, including *A Mighty Fortress Is Our God* and *Away in a Manger*. Throughout the remaining years of his life, Luther continued writing, preaching, and teaching. He died on February 18, 1546, four days after he had preached in Eisleben, his hometown. He was buried on the grounds of the church in Wittenberg.

A caricature of Martin Luther as a seven-headed monster. It was produced after Luther posted his "Ninety-Five Theses" criticizing the Catholic Church. *Reproduced by permission of The Picture Desk.*

For More Information

Books

Fearon, Mike. *Martin Luther*. Minneapolis: Bethany House Publishers, 1986.

Noll, Mark A. *Confessions and Catechisms of the Reformation*. Vancouver, B.C.: Regent College Publishing, 1997.

Scheib, Asta. *Children of Disobedience: The Love Story of Martin Luther and Katharina von Bora: A Novel*. David Ward, translator. New York: Crossroad, 2000.

Stepanek, Sally. *Martin Luther*. New York: Chelsea House, 1986.

Video Recordings

Martin Luther. Worcester, Vision Video, 1990.

Web Sites

"Luther, Martin: Letter to the Archbishop of Mainz, 1517." *Medieval Sourcebook*. [Online] Available http://www.fordham.edu/halsall/source/lutherltr-indulgences.html, April 5, 2002.

"Luther, Martin." *Martin Luther and the Reformation*. [Online] Available http://mars.acnet.wnec.edu/~grempel/courses/wc2/lectures/luther.html, April 5, 2002.

"Luther, Martin." *MSN Encarta*. [Online] Available http://encarta.msn.com/find/concise.asp?z=1&pg=2&ti=04875000, April 5, 2002.

Niccolò Machiavelli

May 3, 1469
Florence, Italy
May 22, 1527
Florence, Italy

Statesman, author

The Italian author and statesman Niccolò Machiavelli is best known as the author of *The Prince* (*Il principe*), in which he described how a ruler must do whatever is necessary to stay in power. Over the centuries Machiavelli became famous as a sinister and ruthless politician because of this philosophy. Many historians suggest that this reputation is largely undeserved. They point out that Machiavelli lived by his own ideals as a loyal and self-sacrificing servant of government. Furthermore, he never suggested that the political dealings of princes should be a model for day-to-day interactions among ordinary citizens.

Niccolò Machiavelli was born into an aristocratic family in Florence, Italy. Though the Machiavellis came from the upper class, they were by no means wealthy. Little is known about the first half of Machiavelli's life prior to his first appointment to public office. His writings show, however, that he was well educated in the classics (works by ancient Greek and Roman writers). Scholars believe he probably knew these works in translations from the original Greek and Latin into his native Italian. They also theorize that his father, who was

" ... how one lives is so far removed from how one ought to live that he who abandons what one does for what one ought to do, learns rather his own ruin than his preservation."

Niccolò Machiavelli,
The Prince.

Niccolò Machiavelli.
©Bettmann/Corbis.
Reproduced by permission
of Corbis Corporation.

a lawyer, had connections in the city that enabled young Machiavelli to meet the important Florentine humanists and literary figures of the time. (Humanists were scholars that promoted the human-centered literary and intellectual movement based on the revival of classical culture that started the Renaissance.) The few known facts of Machiavelli's early life include his friendship with Giulianio de' Medici (1479–1516), brother of the duke of Florence, **Lorenzo de' Medici** (1449–1492; see entry).

Political fortunes rise and fall

In 1498 Machiavelli was named chancellor (head) and secretary of the second chancellery (administrative council) of the Florentine Republic. (A republic is a form of government that is run by representatives of the people and based on a constitution, a document that specifies the rights of citizens and laws of the state.) His duties consisted chiefly of executing the policy decisions of others, conducting diplomatic correspondence, reading and composing reports, and compiling minutes (written records of meetings.) He also undertook some twenty-three missions to states under Florentine rule. He was sent to Pisa, which had rebelled against Florence in 1494, and to the courts of rulers in the unstable Romagna region of north-central Italy. He was twice sent to Imola and Cesena, which were under the leadership of the ruthless military and political leader Cesare Borgia (c. 1475–1507).

In 1503, while on one of these missions, Machiavelli wrote a report titled "Description of the Manner Employed by Duke Valentino [Cesare Borgia] in Slaying Vitellozzo Vitelli, Oliverotto da Fermo, Signor Pagolo and the Duke of Gravina, Orsini," in which he detailed a series of political murders ordered by Borgia. Machiavelli's later writings reveal that encounters with Borgia made a particularly vivid impression on him. His reports to the Florentine government sometimes caused controversy because he did not hesitate to express his own opinions instead of just presenting the facts of his meetings. Examples include his support of an alliance between Florence and the Borgias and his criticism of the Florentine Republic's lack of a local military force. Despite, or perhaps as a result of, his direct approach, Machiavelli won the confidence of Piero Soderini, who was elected *gonfalionier* (head political leader) of Florence in 1502. With Soderini's support, and against the objections of the upper-class families, Machiavelli planned and trained a militia (citizens' army) that played an important role in the reconquest of Pisa in 1509. Also of note from this period were his four diplomatic trips to the French court and two to the court of Rome. In 1502 he married Marietta Corsini, with whom he had four sons and two daughters.

In August 1512 a Spanish army entered Tuscany and raided Prato, a town in the Florentine Republic. Machiavelli's army was no match for the invading forces. Soderini was removed from office and the Medici family was returned to power. (The Medicis had been forced out of Florence when Soderini was elected to office.) The Lorenzo Medici's son, also named Lorenzo and known as Lorenzo the Younger, assumed command of the regime in Florence. On November 7 Machiavelli was dismissed from his post because he had collaborated with Soderini. Machiavelli was ordered to pay a heavy fine and forbidden to travel outside Florentine areas for a full year. The worst came in February 1513, when he was arrested for suspected involvement in a plot against the Medicis. Although there was no evidence that he was involved, he was imprisoned and tortured by Medici supporters who tried to gain incriminating information from him. Machiavelli begged for help from Giuliano de'Medici in a pair of sonnets (type of Italian poetry). Machiavelli was released in March, not through the efforts of Giuliano, but because of a general amnesty (freedom from arrest or criminal charges) declared in celebration of the election of Guiliano's brother, Giovanni (1475–1521), as Pope Leo X (reigned 1513–21). The pope is the supreme head of the Roman Catholic Church. At that time the pope not only controlled the church but he also had great political power.

Turns to writing

Machiavelli's diplomatic career was now finished. He spent much of the next few years in seclusion at his family's country home at Sant'Andrea in Percussina, a few miles south of Florence. His major contact with the outside world was Francesco Vettori, a longtime friend and Florentine diplomat who had been appointed ambassador to the papal (pope's) court. From their correspondence came many of the themes of *The Prince,* which Machiavelli wrote in the second half of 1513. (Many scholars believe the text was significantly changed and expanded in either 1515 to 1516 or 1518.) In 1513 and 1514 he hoped that *The Prince* might find favor with the Medicis and pave the way for his return to political service. Perhaps in an effort to promote his case, Machiavelli first dedicated, or "addressed," the work to Lorenzo the Younger in August 1513. Despite these efforts, the Medicis made clear in early 1515 that they had no intention of employing Machiavelli.

Prior to beginning work on *The Prince* Machiavelli had been writing *Discourses on the First Ten Books of Titus Livius,* which he finished in 1517. Certain passages in this work set forth Machiavelli's quarrel with the church. Here he claimed that the corrupt papal court in Rome had set a bad example and caused Italy to lose its devotion and religion. The Italian states were weak and divided, Machiavelli wrote, because the church was too feeble politically to dominate them, but prevented any one state from uniting them. He suggested that the church might have been completely destroyed by its own corruption had not the Italian priest Saint Francis of Assisi (c. 1181–1226) and the Spanish preacher Saint Dominic (c. 1170–1221) restored it to its original spiritual principles by founding new orders (organizations for religious men and women). Machiavelli's other works include *The Art of War and the Life of Castruccio Castracani* (1520); three plays, *The Mandrake* (1518), *Clizia* (c. 1525), and *Andria* (date uncertain); *History of Florence* (1526); a short story, *Belfagor* (date uncertain); and several minor works in verse and prose.

In *History of Florence* Machiavelli told the story of the Florentine Republic from Lorenzo the Elder's death in 1492 until 1526. Scholars consider it an advance over earlier histories because Machiavelli identified underlying social and political causes rather than merely reporting events. The work was also influential to Machiavelli's political career because he wrote it under a contract from the University of Florence that was approved by Cardinal Giulio de' Medici (1478–1534), soon to be Pope Clement VII (reigned 1523–34). Machiavelli dedicated the work to the pope, perhaps for political reasons. Whether a conscience decision or not, the move worked and opened the door to other opportunities for occasional employment and minor public service, as well as to the publication of the *Art of War* in 1521. During these years Machiavelli and Francesco Guicciardini (1483–1540), Papal Commissary of War in Lombardy, became friends and exchanged some memorable letters. In 1526 Machiavelli was commissioned by Pope Clement VII to inspect the fortifications of Florence. Later that year and in early 1527 Guicciardini employed him in two minor diplomatic missions. In 1527 the Florentines drove the Medicis out one last time and restored the republican constitution, which had been written in 1494 and disbanded 1512. Ironically, Machiavelli's recent involvement with the Medicis made him suspect to the republicans, even though his writings gave the greatest support to republicanism during the Renaissance. Machiavelli died in Florence in 1527, receiving the last rites (ceremony performed upon a person's death) of the church that he had bitterly criticized.

Defined field of politics

Machiavelli is now remembered for the contributions to political theory that he made in *The Prince*. He shared with Renaissance humanists a passion for the revival of ancient literary and spiritual values. To their efforts he added a fierce desire for political and moral renewal on the model of the Roman Republic as depicted by the Roman historians Livy (59 B.C.–A.D. 17) and Tacitus (c. A.D. 56–c. 120). Though a republican at heart, Machiavelli saw the need for a strong political and military leader who could forge a unified state in northern Italy to eliminate French and Spanish domination. Since 1494 France and Spain had been involved in a conflict called the Italian Wars (1494–1559) for control of Italy. When Machiavelli wrote *The Prince* he envisioned the possibility of a strong state while the restored Medicis ruled both Florence, under Lorenzo de' Medici the Younger, and the papacy, under Pope Leo X. Machiavelli had admired Cesare Borgia's energetic creation of a new state in Romagna in the few brief years while Borgia's father, Pope Alexander VI (1431–1503; reigned 1492–1503), occupied the papal throne. The final chapter of *The Prince* is a ringing plea to the Medicis to set Italy free from the French and Spanish "barbarians" (those who lack refinement and culture). It concludes with a quotation from the

Italian poet Petrarch's patriotic poem *Italia mia* (My Italy): "Virtue will take arms against fury, and the battle will be brief; for the ancient valor in Italian hearts is not yet dead." His call fell on deaf ears in 1513 but was to play a role three centuries later.

Machiavelli wrote the twenty-six chapters of *The Prince* in a direct style, using examples from history and current political situations to explain his points. According to scholars, in this work Machiavelli was the first to define politics as a separate field. Up to that time political writers, from the ancients Plato and Aristotle to the fifteenth-century humanists, had treated politics as a branch of morals. This means that they wrote about political life being a mirror of moral life. How the individual person conducted his or her life was a smaller representation of how the society at large should be conducted. Machiavelli's chief innovation was to break with this long tradition and to say that politics is separate from morality. In chapter fifteen of *The Prince* he wrote:

> My intent being to write a useful work for those who understand, it seemed to me more appropriate to pursue the actual truth of the matter than the imagination of it. Many have imagined republics and principalities which were never seen or known really to exist; because how one lives is so far removed from how one ought to live that he who abandons what one does for what one ought to do, learns rather his own ruin than his preservation.

In other words, Machiavelli chose to describe the world as it is rather than as people were taught that it should be.

Central to Machiavelli's view of history and politics are the concepts of *fortuna* (fortune) and *virtù* (virtue). Abandoning the Christian view of history as providential (that is, dictated by God or "providence"), Machiavelli interpreted events in purely human terms. Often it is fortune that gives, or terminates, a political leader's opportunity for decisive action. Machiavelli said that Cesare Borgia, though a great politician, experienced an "extreme malignity of fortune" by falling ill just as his father died. What Machiavelli meant was that God did not decide that the rule of the Borgias should come to an end and therefore caused Cesare to become ill at the time of his father's death. Instead, Machiavelli argued, the Borgias were merely victims of random fortune. Machiavelli

Machiavelli's Ideas Misinterpreted

Over the centuries Machiavelli became famous as a sinister and ruthless politician because of the philosophy he expressed in *The Prince*. Many modern historians have concluded that his ideas were misrepresented by other sixteenth-century writers, and that such a harsh judgment was unfair. The main source of the misrepresentation of Machiavelli's ideas was the English translation, in 1577, of a work called *Contre-Machiavel* (Contrary to Machiavelli) by the French Huguenot (Protestant) writer Gentillet. Gentillet distorted Machiavelli's teachings, which he blamed for the Saint Bartholomew's Day Massacre, the killing of Huguenots in Paris on a church holiday, in 1572. A poem by Gabriel Harvey the following year falsely attributed four principal crimes to Machiavelli: poison, murder, fraud (lying), and violence. The negative image of Machiavelli was popularized by the crafty and greedy villain Machiavel in *The Jew of Malta* (1588), a play by the English playwright Christopher Marlowe. Machiavellian villains followed in works by other playwrights as well.

wrote that Moses, Cyrus, Romulus, and Theseus also received opportunities for leadership from fortune. In drawing comparisons among these religious and political figures, Machiavelli asserted that sacred (religious or biblical) history was influenced by the same forces as secular (nonreligious) history.

In some passages of *The Prince* Machiavelli seems to suggest that fortune itself hinges upon human actions and institutions: "I believe that the fortune which the Romans had would be enjoyed by all princes who proceeded as the Romans did and who were of the same virtue as they." Like others during Renaissance, Machiavelli believed in the capacity of human beings to determine their own destiny. This was different from the medieval concept of an omnipotent, or almighty, divine will or the ancient Greek belief in a crushing fate. Machiavelli also claimed that virtù in politics, unlike Christian virtue (capacity for doing good), is an effective combination of force and shrewdness with a touch of greatness. Therefore, virtue is not a system of ethical behavior that is outlined in the Scriptures or determined by the church, but instead it is the result of a person's own desire and actions, which then lead to greatness.

The main points of *The Prince* are found in chapter seventeen titled "On Cruelty and Clemency and Whether It Is Better To Be Loved or Feared," and in chapter eighteen, "How Princes Should Keep Their Word." As Machiavelli frequently says in other works as well, the natural badness of men requires that the prince instill fear rather than love in his subjects. Furthermore, when necessary the prince must break his pledge with other princes, who in any case will be no more honest than he. Moralistic critics of Machiavelli have sometimes forgotten that he was attempting to describe rather than to invent the rules of political success. For him the state is an organism, greater than the sum of its citizens and individual interests, which is subject to laws of growth and decay. He claimed that the health of the state consists in unity, but even in the best of circumstances its longevity is limited.

The influence of *The Prince* on political developments in Europe, especially during the nineteenth century, cannot be overemphasized. Many of Machiavelli's concepts formed the basis of nineteenth-century liberalism, a political philosophy that advocates change for the good of the state and its citizens. Among these concepts were the supremacy of civil over religious power, requiring men to serve in citizen armies, the preference for republican rather than monarchical government, the Roman republican ideals of honesty and hard work, and people's ultimate responsibility to their community, not simply to themselves. *The Prince* remains one of the most important political writings of Western (non-Asian) civilization.

For More Information

Books

Skinner, Quentin. *Great Political Thinkers*. New York: Oxford University Press, 1992.

Vergani, Luis. *"The Prince." Notes; Including Machiavelli's Life and Works*. Lincoln, Nebr.: Cliff's Notes, 1967.

Viroli, Maurizio. *Niccolò's Smile: A Biography of Machiavelli*. Antony Shugaar, translator. New York: Farrar, Straus and Giroux, 2000.

Web Sites

"Machiavelli, Nicolo." *Internet Philosophy Encyclopedia*. [Online] Available http://www.utm.edu/research/iep/m/machiave.htm, April 5, 2002.

"Machiavelli, Nicolo," *MSN Encarta*. [Online] Available http://encarta.msn.com/find/Concise.asp?ti=05DD9000, April 5, 2002.

Margaret of Navarre

**April 11, 1492
Cognac, France
December 21, 1549
Odos-Bigorre, France**

Writer

M argaret of Navarre, duchess of Angoulême, is best known today as the author of *Heptaméron*. A collection of novellas (a form of short fictitious stories originating in Italy), *Heptaméron* is ranked alongside the books of **François Rabelais** (c. 1494–1553; see entry) and **Michel de Montaigne** (1533–1592; see entry) as one of the greatest prose works of the French Renaissance. The Renaissance was a cultural revolution that began in Italy in the mid-1300s. It was initiated by scholars called humanists who promoted the human-centered values of ancient Greece and Rome. Humanist ideals were soon influencing the arts, literature, philosophy, science, religion, and politics in Italy. During the early fifteenth century, innovations of the Italian Renaissance began spreading into the rest of Europe and reached a peak in the sixteenth century.

"… and I will tell you nothing but the whole truth."

Simontault in Heptaméron.

Margaret of Navarre.
©*Archivo Iconografico, S. A./Corbis. Reproduced by permission of Corbis Corporation.*

Influential at brother's court

Margaret was born at Cognac, France, in 1492, the daughter of Charles de Valois (died 1496), count of

Heptaméron: Day the First

Heptaméron is considered one of the great works of French Renaissance literature. It consists of seventy-two tales that are narrated by five noblemen and five noblewomen who are stranded by a flood. They have decided to tell stories while waiting for a bridge to be built. After each story, they comment on the tale just told. One of the men, a knight named Simontault, opens the narrative on the first day with a tale about "the bad turns done by women to men, and by men to women." He tells of the "misdeeds of the wife of a certain proctor [clergyman], who had a bishop for her gallant [lover]."

Simontault's tale begins:

Fair ladies, I have had such a poor reward for all my long service that, to avenge me on Love, and her whose heart is so hard toward me, I am about to recount to you the misdeeds done of women on us poor men; and I will tell you nothing but the whole truth.

In the town of Alençon, in the time of the last Duke Charles, there was a proctor named St. Aignan, who had for wife a gentlewoman of the country. And she, having more beauty than virtue, and being of fickle disposition, was courted by the Bishop of Séez, who, to gain his ends, handled the husband in such fashion that he not only did not perceive the wickedness of the Bishop, but did even forget the love he had for his master [Duke Charles] and mistress [the duchess, Duke Charles's wife], and at last had dealings with wizards [magicians], that thereby he might compass [cause] the death of the duchess. For a long while did the Bishop have dalliance with this evil woman, who received him not for the love she bore him, but because her husband, being greedy of money, so charged her. But her love she gave to a

Angoulême, and Louise of Savoy (1476–1531). Margaret's father was a cousin of the king of France, Louis XII (1462–1515; ruled 1498–1515). Margaret and her brother Francis, the future **Francis I** (1494–1547; see entry), king of France, were brought up at Cognac by their mother, who supervised their education. In 1507 Margaret and Francis left their mother's household to live at the court of Louis XII. Eight years later Francis took the throne and Margaret became an important political and social figure. In 1527, two years after the death of her first husband, Margaret married Henry II (1503–1555; ruled 1517–55), king of Navarre. Interested in religious and philosophical matters, she had read the Bible (the Christian holy book) and the works of Italian poets Dante (Dante Alighieri; 1265–1321) and **Petrarch** (1304–1374; see entry).

young man of Alençon, son of the lieu-tenant-general, and him she loved to mad-ness; often obtaining of the Bishop to send her husband away, that she might see Du Mesnil, the son of the lieutenant, at her ease. And this fashion of life lasted a long while, she having the Bishop for profit, and Du Mesnil for pleasure, for she told the last [Du Mesnil] that all the pleas-aunce [pleasure] she did to the Bishop was but for his sake, and that from her the Bishop only got words, and he might rest assured that no man beside himself got aught [anything] else.

The woman's trickery has tragic consequences. Her husband, St. Aignan, hires a man to kill her lover, Du Mesnil. St. Aignan flees with her to England, but even-tually they return to France. St. Aignan then hires a wizard named Gallery to cast a spell that will bring about the deaths of the duke, the duchess, and his wife because they know the truth about the murder of Du Mesnil. The plot is uncovered, however, and St. Aignan and Gallery are put on trial. The court has mercy on them because they were manipulated by St. Aignan's wife. The wife continues to sin and meets a just fate by dying a miserable death.

At the conclusion of the tale Si-montault challenges an aged widow, Mis-tress Oisille, to tell a story about a virtuous woman, if one can be found. Oisille gladly takes the challenge, saying, "And since there is come to my mind the recollection of a woman well worthy of being had in everlasting remembrance, I will tell you her history." So begins the second tale.

Source: Margaret of Navarre. Heptaméron. *Arthur Machen, translator. New York: E. P. Dutton, 1905, pp. 11, 18.*

Margaret set the intellectual and cultural tone at court, especially in the 1530s and early 1540s. Although a supporter of reform in the Roman Catholic Church, the only established Christian religion at the time, Margaret remained outwardly obedient to Catholicism. At the same time, however, she pro-tected leading reformers such as Guillaume Briçonnet (c. 1472–1534) and Jacques d'Ètaples Lefèvre (c. 1455–1536), who were suspected of advocating Lutheranism. Lutheranism was a religious reform movement led by the German priest **Martin Luther** (1483–1546; see entry), which later resulted in the Protestant Reformation and the formation of a Christian reli-gion that is separate from Roman Catholicism.

Margaret was a prolific writer and produced many works, though few were published during her lifetime. In

1531 she published the long poem *Le miroir de l'âme pécheresse* (Mirror of the sinful soul), which was followed two years later by *Dialogue en forme de vision nocturne* (Dialogue in the form of a nocturnal vision). These works were condemned by the theology faculty (professors of religion) at the Sorbonne, a college in Paris, because of Margaret's reformist views concerning grace (virtue coming from God), faith (belief in God), and free will (freedom of humans to make choices without God's assistance). In 1547 she published a collection of her poetry under the title of *Les marguerites de la marguerite des princesses* (Pearls from the pearl of princesses).

Heptaméron is classic work

Margaret's most famous work is *Heptaméron*. Published in 1458, nine years after her death, the book contains seventy-two tales. Margaret modeled it on *Decameron,* a popular book by the medieval Italian writer Giovanni Boccaccio (1313–1375). The narrative takes place over seven days, with ten stories on each day. Two tales are told on an eighth day, but Margaret died before she completed her manuscript. She had planned one hundred stories to be told in ten days, like *Decameron*. The narrative centers on ten aristocrats—five men and five women—who are stranded by a flood. They decide to tell stories while waiting for a bridge to be built. After each story, they comment on the tale just told, drawing from it moral lessons that usually present contradictions and have no neat conclusions. Complex relationships are established among the speakers. They focus on the difficulties of meeting the demands of a worldly life while trying to live according to the Christian message of charity. Because of the frank and stark depiction of sexual desire, many sixteenth-century readers were perplexed by the book and tended to view it as a collection of indecent tales. Late-twentieth-century scholars reevaluated *Heptaméron,* however, stressing its complex narrative and the prominence of women in the tales. The book is now considered a classic of the French Renaissance.

For More Information

Books

Marguerite de Navarre. *The Heptaméron.* P.A. Chilton, translator. New York: Penguin Books, 1984.

Web Sites

The Heptameron of Margaret, Queen of Navarre. [Online] Available http://digital.library.upenn.edu/women/navarre/heptameron/heptameron.html, April 5, 2002.

"Margaret of Angoulême." *Britannica.com.* [Online] Available http://www.britannica.com/seo/m/margaret-of-angouleme, April 5, 2002.

"Margaret of Navarre." *Infoplease.com.* [Online] Available http://www.infoplease.com/ce6/people/A0831778.html, April 5, 2002.

Lorenzo de' Medici

January 1, 1449
Florence, Italy
April 9, 1492
Florence, Italy

Merchant

The Italian merchant prince Lorenzo de' Medici, called "il Magnifico" ("the Magnificent"), ruled both the Florentine state and a vast commercial empire. As a poet and a patron, or financial supporter, of poets, he stimulated the revival and splendor of Italian literature.

Lorenzo de' Medici was born in Florence, Italy, on January 1, 1449. He was the son of Piero the Gouty (1414–1469) and the grandson of Cosimo the Elder (1389–1464). His mother, Lucrezia Tornabuoni, was also an accomplished poet. Cosimo was aware of his son Piero's physical weakness and fearful that Piero would not long survive him. He therefore groomed his grandson Lorenzo to become a merchant and take over the family business. Lorenzo enjoyed the best education available, learning Greek, Latin, and philosophy (search for a general understanding of values and reality through speculative thinking). He received both a formal education, in rigorous sessions with teachers, and an informal one, in the company of humanists (scholars who promoted the human-centered literary and intellectual movement based on the revival of classical culture that started the Re-

Lorenzo de' Medici.

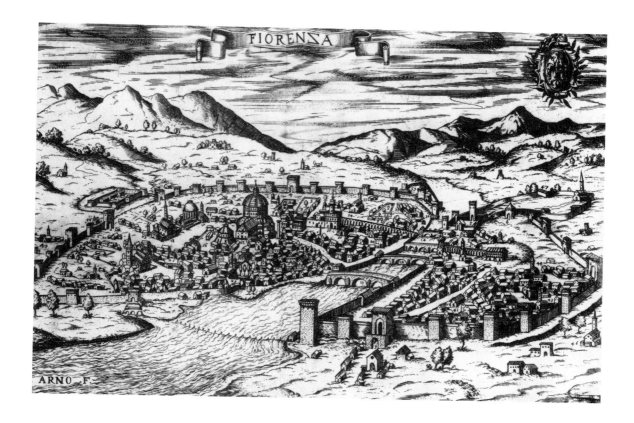

FIORENZA

ARNO F

naissance) and statesmen. While still a youth, he began to write poetry, usually about love. In 1469, on his father's advice, he married Clarice Orsini, a woman who belonged to one of the oldest, most powerful noble families of Rome.

Becomes ruler of Florence

Piero died on December 5, 1469, and two days later the twenty-year-old Lorenzo was asked by a delegation (committee) of eminent citizens to take control of the city-state of Florence. This he did, ruling as his father and grandfather had done, from behind the scenes and without holding any public office. In 1471 Lorenzo increased the prestige and stability of his family. He made an agreement with Pope Sixtus IV (1414–1484; reigned 1471–84), head of the Roman Catholic Church (a Christian religion based in Rome, Italy), by which the Medicis would continue to handle the finances of the papacy (office of the pope). The following year he won the

The walled city of Florence, Italy. After his father's death Lorenzo was asked by a delegation of eminent citizens to take control of the city-state. *Reproduced by permission of Hulton Archive.*

hearts of all Florentines by saving the city from an imminent famine. When the bad harvest of that year threatened the population with disaster, it was Lorenzo who imported large amounts of grain.

Although it was always central to Medici policy to retain close ties with the Holy See (office of the pope), relations between Lorenzo and Pope Sixtus were not always friendly. The pope was displeased when Lorenzo's diplomacy (political negotiations) achieved an alliance between Florence, Venice, and Milan. As ruler of the Papal States (territory controlled by the pope), Sixtus thought that such a combination was more than a match for the armies of the church, which indeed they were. Sixtus felt his ambitions to expand the papal territory had been ruined and was uneasy about the safety of the territory already under the control of the church. His hostility grew when he learned that Lorenzo was trying to buy the town of Imola, which was strategically important to anyone who was trying to seize the surrounding territory. Consequently the pope approved a plot designed to rid Florence of both Lorenzo and his brother Giuliano (1479–1516). The chief conspirators were the Pazzi family, a rival banking house and bitter enemies of the Medicis. The plan was to assassinate the two brothers at a moment when their guard would be down, during the celebration of mass on Easter Sunday, April 26, 1478. (Mass is a Catholic worship service. Easter is the Christian celebration of the day when Jesus of Nazareth, the founder of Christianity, rose from the dead after being crucified.) Giuliano was slain, but Lorenzo escaped with just wounds. The people of Florence rallied to the side of the Medicis and unleashed terrible revenge on the conspirators, most of whom did not survive the day. Among those killed was Francesco Salviato, archbishop (head of a church district) of Pisa.

The enraged pope excommunicated (expelled) Lorenzo from membership in the church and placed an interdict on the city. (An interdict is a papal order that removes the right of church sacraments, such as marriage and burial, from the citizens of a district.) In 1479, in the midst of unbearable tension, Sixtus and King Ferdinand I (1423–1494; ruled 1458–94) of Naples declared war on Florence. Lorenzo, knowing that the safety of his city and his dynasty were at stake, undertook the most hazardous adventure of his colorful career. Virtually placing his life in the hands of Ferdinand, Lorenzo went to Naples to meet with the king. Ferdinand was won over by Lorenzo's charm and his persuasive argument that it would not do for Italy to be divided or for Florence to be destroyed. Lorenzo returned to Florence with the gift of peace and was received with great joy. Sixtus was bitter but grudgingly made peace with Lorenzo in 1480. This was the last time that Lorenzo's control over Florence and its possessions would be challenged.

In the political arena Lorenzo appeared to have done everything possible to secure the future of his family line. His eldest son and heir, Piero (1471–1503), was trained by his father as a political leader and patron of the arts. In 1487 Piero was married to Alfonsina Orsini, an alliance that renewed the important tie with the family of Lorenzo's wife Clarice. Most important to Lorenzo's plans was a friendly relationship with Pope Innocent VIII (1432–1492; reigned 1484–92). In 1486 Lorenzo negotiated peace in the Baron's War between the papacy and Ferdinand of Naples. He then arranged the marriage of his daughter Maddalena to the pope's nephew, Franceschetto Cibò. In 1488 Lorenzo's son Giovanni (1475–1521) was named a cardinal deacon of the church of Santa Maria in Dominica, at the unheard-of age of thirteen. Giovanni later became Pope Leo X (reigned 1513–21). Only in the management of the Medici bank, which suffered large losses in the 1480s and 1490s, can Lorenzo be said to have failed in providing for his heirs.

Patronizes Renaissance culture

The private fortune of the Medicis declined under Lorenzo's management, primarily because he tended to neglect personal business in favor of diplomatic and cultural concerns.

 Council of Seventy

A new constitution in 1480 simplified the structure of Florentine government. The Signory, or executive branch, chose thirty citizens, who in turn selected forty more, all to serve for life on a new council. It was called the Council of Seventy. From that time forward all other branches, including the Signory, were responsible to the permanent Council of Seventy. Since the council was filled with Lorenzo's supporters, the effect of the constitutional change was to make his tyranny more obvious. Under this rule the prosperity of Florence grew, primarily in banking and commerce. Lorenzo contributed greatly to this prosperity through the peace that his diplomacy secured from 1480 until his death in 1492.

It is not accidental that the last decade of his life coincided with the period of Florence's greatest artistic contributions to the Renaissance. Lorenzo commissioned works by painters Sandro Botticelli (1445–1510), Domenico Ghirlandaio (1449–1494), and Fra Filippo Lippi (1457–1504) to add beauty to the city. The humanist John Lascaris (c. 1445–c. 1535) and the poet Angelo Poliziano (1454–1494) traveled long distances at the request and the expense of Lorenzo in search of manuscripts to enlarge the Medici libraries. What could not be bought was copied, and Lorenzo permitted the scribes (those who copy texts) of other eager book collectors to copy from his manuscripts. When Poliziano and others scorned the new invention of printing from movable type (see **Johannes Gutenberg** entry), Lorenzo had the foresight to recognize its value and encourage its use. The famous Platonic Academy frequently met at Lorenzo's palace, where in lively philosophic discussions the ruler was the equal of humanist **Giovanni Pico della Mirandola** (1463–1494; see entry), painter and architect **Michelangelo** (1475–1564; see entry), and philosopher Marsilio Ficino (1433–1499). The University of Pisa owes it revival to Lorenzo.

Lorenzo was also an important patron of sculpture, architecture, and music. He commissioned two bronze statues, probably *Boy With Fish* and *David,* from Andreas del Verrocchio (1435–1488) for his villa at Careggi. He also provided stimulus to public and ecclesiastic (religious) projects. Among them was a plan for neighborhood renewal in the quarter of San Giovanni. He financed Verocchio's work on the tombs of Piero and Diovanni de' Medici in San Lorenxo. He also commissioned the building of a monastery (house for monks, members of a religious order) for the Augustinian Observants (a religious order) at San Gallo, and sponsored a competition to design a cathedral facade (front wall). In music Lorenzo was influenced from an early age by Antonio Squarcialupi, who asked an important composer to set one of Lorenzo's verses to music. Lorenzo also brought Flemish composer Heinrich Isaac (1450–1517) to Florence, where he became musical tutor to the Medici children.

Revives Tuscan Italian

The many feats of patronage touched upon here, though significant, are secondary on the scale of Lorenzo's accomplishments. He made a major contribution to Italian poetry by writing verses in Tuscan Italian, the language spoken by natives of Tuscany. The Italian poet Dante (1265–1321), the first to write in Italian, had elevated Tuscan Italian to the status of a literary language. Then the humanists buried it under mounds of classical Latin. Although his friend Poliziano still favored Latin, Lorenzo composed Italian poems that compared favorably with other verse written in his time. He has been credited with restoring the Tuscan dialect (spoken form of a language) to its previous status. Lorenzo's *canti carnascialeschi* (carnival songs) are still read with pleasure.

Lorenzo was not known for his physical attractiveness, yet his dignity, charm, and wit came from his manner rather than his appearance. He had a reputation for immorality in both his personal life and business practices, but this did not prevent him from being loved and admired. Lorenzo died at his villa at Careggi on April 8, 1492, almost certainly of gout (painful inflammation of the joints). His doctor was accused of negligence and thrown into a well. Flemish composer Heinrich Isaac (c. 1450–1517) wrote music performed at Lorenzo's funeral. A death mask (plaster mold made from the face of a dead person) of Lorenzo can still be seen.

For More Information

Books

Ripley, Alexandra. *The Time Returns*. Garden City, N.Y.: Doubleday, 1985.

Shulman, Sandra. *The Florentine*. New York, N.Y.: Morrow, 1973.

Web Sites

Medici Family, The. [Online] Available http://es.rice.edu/ES/humsoc/Galileo/People/medici.html, April 5, 2002.

"Medici, Lorenzo de', 1492–1519—Italian merchant prince." *Infoplease.com.* [Online] Available http://www.infoplease.com/ce6/people/A0832477.html, April 5, 2002.

Michelangelo Buonarroti

March 6, 1475
Caprese, Italy
February 18, 1564
Rome, Italy

Artist

Michelangelo Buonarroti (known as Michelangelo) was the greatest sculptor of the Italian Renaissance. He was also one of the greatest painters and architects of the time. In fact, Michelangelo had an exceptionally long career and dominated the Renaissance. The Renaissance was a movement based on the revival of ancient Greek and Roman culture (the classical period). When he died in 1564, at age eighty-nine, he had lived nearly twice the expected life span of the average person in the sixteenth century. His impact on younger artists was immense, but it tended to be crushing. Major artists of the next century, such as **Peter Paul Rubens** (1577–1640; see entry), were better able to study Michelangelo's ideas at a distance without danger to their own artistic independence.

Begins sculpting

Michelangelo was born in Caprese, an Italian village where his father, Ludovico di Leonardo Buonarroti Simoni, briefly served as an agent for the government of Florence. The family had been in the banking business and therefore had a

Michelangelo Buonarroti.

higher social rank than that of other artists' families in Florence. In the sixteenth century artists were still considered craftsmen—they belonged to trade guilds (associations of craftsmen, merchants, and professionals that trained apprentices and set standards of production or business operation), as did skilled laborers such as shoemakers or carpenters—and they were on the same social level as common workers. Michelangelo's grandfather had failed as a banker, however, and his father was too genteel to go into trade. Consequently, the family lived on the income from land and his father's few official appointments. His mother died when he was six. After completing grammar school, Michelangelo was apprenticed at age thirteen to Domenico Ghirlandaio (Domenico di Tommaso Bigordi; 1449–1494), the most fashionable painter in Florence. The apprenticeship was broken off within a year, and Michelangelo was given access to the collection of ancient Roman sculpture owned by **Lorenzo de' Medici** (1449–1492; see entry), duke of Florence. The boy dined with the Medici family and was looked after by the retired sculptor who was in charge of the collection. This arrangement was quite unprecedented at the time.

Michelangelo began working as a sculptor in 1492, at age seventeen. Over the next sixteen years he produced many of the best-known sculptures of the Italian Renaissance. His earliest sculpture was a stone relief (raised images on a flat background) titled *Battle of the Centaurs,* which was based on a Latin poem a court poet read to him. Resembling the Roman sarcophagi (coffins) in the Medici collection, it had simple, solid forms and squarish figures that added intensity to their violent interaction. Soon after Lorenzo de' Medici died in 1492, the Medicis fell from power and Michelangelo fled from Florence to Bologna. In 1494 he obtained a commission to carve three saints needed to complete the tomb of Saint Dominic in the church of San Domenico. The tomb had been started by the sculptor Nicola Pisano (c. 1220–1278 or 1284) around 1265. In this work Michelangelo's figures are again squarish, in contrast with the linear forms that were then dominant in sculpture.

After settling in Rome in 1496, Michelangelo made a statue of Bacchus, the Greek god of wine, for the garden of ancient sculpture owned by a banker. His earliest surviving large-scale work, *Bacchus* shows the god in a teetering stance, either because he is drunk or dancing. It is Michelangelo's only sculpture meant to be viewed from all sides. His other works were generally set in front of walls and to some extent resemble reliefs. In 1498, through the same banker, Michelangelo obtained his first important commission, the larger-than-life *Pietà,* which is now in Saint Peter's Basilica, the largest church in the Christian world and the symbol of papal authority. The term *pietà* refers to a popular image in which Mary (mother of Jesus Christ, founder of Christianity) supports the dead Christ across her knees. Although several versions of this scene have been created, Michelangelo's sculpture is the most famous. In both the *Pietà* and the *Bacchus* he made hard polished marble resemble soft flesh.

Known as greatest sculptor

When Michelangelo returned to Florence in 1501, he was recognized as the most talented sculptor in central Italy. That year he was commissioned to do the marble sculpture *David* for Florence Cathedral. After he completed the project in 1504, it was placed in front of the Palazzo Vecchio. Immediately thereafter Michelangelo accepted the job of painting the *Battle of Cascina,* a huge fresco (wall painting) for the Council Chamber of the Republic in the Palazzo della Signoria. The building was to have vast patriotic murals that would also show the special skills of Florence's two leading artists: **Leonardo da Vinci** (1452–1529; see entry) and Michelangelo.

The subject of Michelangelo's fresco, the Battle of Cascina, was a celebrated Florentine military victory. Although Michelangelo never completed this fresco, several sketches and a copy of the cartoon (design plan) exist. (At that time a cartoon had not yet come to mean a satirical or humorous drawing. Instead, it was a preparatory design or drawing for a fresco.) The central scene shows a group of muscular nude soldiers climbing from a river where they had been swimming to answer a military alarm. This work clearly showed Leonardo's influence in the depiction of a continuous flowing motion through living forms. This combination of throbbing life with colossal grandeur became the special quality of Michelangelo's art. From then on his work consisted mainly of very large projects that he never finished. Because

he preferred to work on a grand scale, however, he could not turn down commissions from great clients. For instance, he contracted to make statues of the Twelve Apostles (Jesus Christ's disciples) for the Florence Cathedral, yet he started only the *St. Matthew*.

Michelangelo had stopped working on the Apostle statues when Pope Julius II (1443–1513; reigned 1503–13)

The Creation **painted by Michelangelo on the ceiling of the Sistine Chapel.**

called him to Rome in 1505. He had accepted a commission to design the pope's tomb, which was to include about forty life-size statues. This project occupied him off and on for the next forty years. In 1506 a dispute over funds for the tomb led Michelangelo, who had spent almost a year at the marble quarries (sites where marble is extracted from the ground) in Carrara, to flee to Florence. A reconciliation between Julius II and Michelangelo later took place in Bologna, which the pope had just conquered.

Paints Sistine ceiling

Michelangelo's career took another direction in 1508, when Pope Julius II offered him a commission to decorate the ceiling of the Sistine Chapel at the Vatican in Rome. At first Michelangelo protested that he was a sculptor, not a painter. Finally he accepted the job and devoted all of his creative energies to the project. The theme of the ceiling painting is the nine stories from the book of Genesis in the Bible. Interspersed with figures of the male biblical prophets (Hebrew leaders) are the female sibyls (prophetesses) of antiquity, a series of nude youths, lunettes (crescent-shaped decorative objects) with representations of the ancestors of Christ, and a host of other figures and decoration.

By the time the Sistine Chapel project was completed four years later, in 1512, Michelangelo had made a major innovation in ceiling painting. Traditionally, artists had depicted only single figures, but he introduced the portrayal of dramatic scenes involving hundreds of figures. The concept was so successful that it set the standard for future artists. The painting is also considered one of the most awe-inspiring works of Western (non-Asian) art. The German poet Johann Wolfgang von Goethe (1749–1832) reportedly remarked that one cannot fully appreciate human achievement without first seeing the Sistine Chapel. Nevertheless, the project had been a grueling one for Michelangelo. He was required to lie on a scaffold with arms outstretched for hours at a time. As a result of working on the Sistine Chapel, he was reportedly disabled for the rest of his life. An accomplished and prolific poet, Michelangelo composed "Sonnet to John of Pistoia on the Sistine Ceiling" (1509–12). The first two stanzas, as quoted in

The Complete Poems of Michelangelo translated by John Frederick Nims, give the reader an idea of the physical stress and pain he endured for four years:

> I've got myself a goiter [enlarged thyroid gland] from this
>   strain,
> As water gives the cats in Lombardy
> Or maybe it is in some other country;
> My belly's pushed by force beneath my chin.
> My beard toward Heaven, I feel the back of my brain
> Upon my neck, I grow the breast of a Harpy [Greek mytho-
>   logical creature];
> My brush, above my face continually,
> Makes it a splendid floor by dripping down.

Michelangelo concluded the poem with this line: "I'm not in a good place, and I'm no painter."

Favored by popes

As soon as the Sistine ceiling was completed, Michelangelo returned to the tomb of Julius and carved *Moses* and *Slaves.* Julius's death in 1513 halted the work on his tomb. For the next few years Michelangelo created sculptures for popes. They were anxious to have work by the recognized greatest sculptor of monuments for themselves, their families, and the church. Pope Leo X (1475–1521; reigned 1513–21), son of Lorenzo de' Medici, proposed a marble facade for the family parish church of Saint Lorenzo in Florence. It was to be decorated with statues by Michelangelo, but the project was canceled after four years of quarrying and designing.

In 1520 Michelangelo was commissioned to execute a tomb chapel for two young Medici dukes. The Medici Chapel (1520–34), an annex to Saint Lorenzo, is the most nearly complete large sculptural project of Michelangelo's career. The two tombs, each with an image of the deceased and two allegorical figures (images of people with symbolic significance), are placed against elaborately decorated walls. These six statues and a seventh, the *Madonna,* on a third wall are by Michelangelo's own hand. The two saints flanking the *Madonna* were made by assistants from his clay sketches. The allegories on the curved lids of the tombs are also innovative: *Day and Night* recline on one tomb, *Morning and Evening* on the other. Political leaders were becoming more powerful at the time, and

Bramante Designs New Saint Peter's

Donato di Pascuccio d'Antonio (called Bramante; 1444–1514) was the first influential Renaissance architect. He introduced a grave and monumental style that represented the ideal for later architects.

Bramante was born at Monte Asdruvaldo near Urbino. Little is known about his life until the late 1470s. Around 1481 he was named court architect for the Sforza family, the rulers of Lombardy. Bramante's first important commissions were for various features of churches in Milan. He fled to Rome in 1499, when the French captured Milan in 1499, during the Italian Wars (1494–1559; a conflict between France and Spain over control of Italy). After the election of Pope Julius II in 1503, Bramante became the official papal architect. He did extensive work in the Vatican Palace. In 1505 Pope Julius II decided that Saint Peter's Basilica should be completely rebuilt, and he commissioned Bramante to prepare a plan for the new church. Bramante based his plan on a central Greek cross design (an upright shaft crossed in the middle by a shaft of equal length). It called for a large dome sitting atop a drum (open circular base) supported by colonnades at the crossing. It also featured four smaller domes and corner towers.

When the Greek-cross design was not accepted, Bramante planned to lengthen one arm of the cross to form a nave (main part of a church) and thus suggest the shape of a Latin cross (a long shaft crossed with a shorter shaft above the middle). He then added ambulatories (walk-

Michelangelo's statues were often used as models for portraits that depicted emperors, popes, kings, and dukes.

Paints Reformation works

In 1534 Michelangelo left Florence for the last time and settled in Rome. For the next ten years he produced paintings for Pope Paul III (1468–1549; reigned 1534–49). The pope had convened a series of meetings called the Council of Trent, which initiated the Catholic Reformation, a wide-ranging effort to revitalize the Roman Catholic Church. One area of reform was the arts, through which Paul III wanted to promote a more human image of the church. The first project Michelangelo executed for the pope was the *Last Judgment* (1536–41), a vast painting on the end wall of the Sistine

ways) in the wings that projected outward from the center of the cross. The foundation stone was laid in 1506, but at the time of his death Bramante had erected only the four main piers (bases) and the arches that were to support the dome. In 1513 the pope bestowed the office of *Piombatore,* or sealer of the papal briefs, on Bramante. The architect's last work was probably the Palazzo Caprini, which he started after 1510. Later owned by Italian architect Raphael, the Palazzo Caprini became the model for numerous palaces, especially in northern Italy. Bramante died in 1514 and was buried in Old Saint Peter's Basilica.

Bramante's design for the new Saint Peter's continued to cause controversy throughout the sixteenth century. Many critics wanted the church to have a more pronounced Latin-cross structure. Raphael and Bramante's assistant Antonio da Sangallo (1483–1546), changed the design and construction was delayed. Michelangelo took over the project in 1547. When he died in 1564, the building was completed in its present form up to the dome. Giacomo della Porta (c. 1537–1602) then altered the design again (he may have used a model made by Michelangelo) and completed the dome in 1590. Finally, supporters of the Latin cross design won, and the architect Carlo Maderna (1556–1629) added a nave and facade, which were completed in 1614.

Chapel. The design functions like a pair of scales, with some angels pushing the damned (those who have not been forgiven for their sins) to hell on one side and some pulling up the saved (those whose sins have been forgiven) on the other side. Angels on both sides are directed by Christ, who "conducts" with both arms. In the two top corners are the cross (Christ died on a cross in order to save all of humankind) and other symbols of the Passion (the crucifixion and death of Christ), which serve as Christ's credentials to be judge.

In the *Last Judgment* Michelangelo used simple colors, blue and brown. The somber tone seems to parallel the ideas of the Catholic Reformation, which called for a renewed emphasis on spirituality. Michelangelo had contact with reform leaders through the poet Vittoria Colonna (1492–1547), a close friend and supporter to whom he addressed many of his poems. From 1541 until 1545 Michelangelo painted two large frescoes—*Conversion of Saul* and *Crucifixion of Peter*—for the Pauline Chapel in the Vatican. They are similar to the *Last Judgment,* but in these works he expressed movement through linear perspective (a technique that depicts a scene from a single point of view; see **Leonardo** entry). He also used subtle colors in a more expressive way. He may have turned to these techniques because the Pauline Chapel frescoes were the first ones he executed on a normal scale and at eye level. Michelangelo's only sculpture during this period was limited to two pietàs that he executed for himself. The first one (unfinished), which is in the Cathedral of Florence, was meant for his own tomb. His last sculpture was the *Rondanini Pietà* in Milan, which he started in 1555 and was working on just six days prior to his death in 1564.

Concentrates on architecture

After 1545 Michelangelo devoted himself almost entirely to architecture. He had been working on architectural commissions since 1538, when Paul III commissioned him to redesign and refurbish Capitoline Hill, the geographical and ceremonial center of ancient Rome. As with many of Michelangelo's other commissions, the project was completed after his death. Paul III also hired him to direct construction of the Farnese Palace in 1546. During the reign of Pius IV (1499–1565; reigned 1559–65) Michelangelo designed the Porta Pia, converted the Roman Baths of Diocletion into the Christian church of Santa Maria segli Angeli, and designed the Sforza Chapel in Santa Maria Maggiore. Thus Michelangelo became an urban planner as well as an architect, helping to transform the appearance of Rome.

In 1547 Paul III appointed Michelangelo to direct construction of the new Saint Peter's Basilica. The project had been beset by problems since 1506, when Pope Julius II originally ordered the rebuilding of the Old Saint Peter's. By the time Michelangelo took over the project more than forty years later, three other architects—Bramante (see accompanying box), **Raphael** (1483–1520; see entry), and Antonio da Sangallo (1483–1546)—had changed the design, and construction was delayed. When Michelangelo died in 1564 the building was completed in its present form up to the dome. Two other architects, Giacomo della Porta (c. 1537–1602) and Carlo Maderna (1556–1629), worked on the church before its completion in 1614. Saint Peter's is now considered the crowning achievement of Renaissance architecture.

Further Reading

Books

The Complete Poems of Michelangelo. John Frederick Nims, translator. Chicago, Ill.: University of Chicago Press, 1998.

Stanley, Diane. *Michelangelo.* New York: HarperCollins, 2000.

Video Recordings

The Agony and the Ecstasy. Livonia, Mich.: CBS/Fox Video, 1988.

Masterpieces of Italian Art, Volume: Da Vinci, Michelangelo, Raphael and Titian. New York: VPI-AC Video Inc., 1990.

Web Sites

Kren, Emil, and Daniel Marx. "Michelangelo." *Web Gallery of Art.* [Online] Available http://www.kfki.hu/~arthp/html/m/michelan/, April 5, 2002.

"Michelangelo." *MSN Encarta.* [Online] Available http://encarta.msn.com/find/Concise.asp?z=1&pg=2&ti=761560125, April 5, 2002.

Michelangelo—Sistine Chapel Ceiling. [Online] Available http://www.science.wayne.edu/~mcogan/Humanities/Sistine/index.html, April 5, 2002.

Pioch, Nicolas. "Michelangelo." *WebMuseum.* [Online] Available http://www.puc-rio.br/wm/paint/auth/michelangelo/, April 5, 2002.

Michel de Montaigne

February 23, 1533
Périgord, France
September 13, 1592
Bordeaux, France

Author

Michel de Montaigne.

The French author Michel de Montaigne created a new literary genre (form), the essay, in which he used self-portrayal as a mirror of humanity in general. The term "essay" was first used by Montaigne for short prose discussions. It comes from the French word *essai,* meaning "trial," "an attempt," or "testing." The informal essay as Montaigne understood and developed it is the method a writer uses to test his or her own views on life and the self.

Begins publishing career

Michel de Montaigne was born into a noble, or upperclass, family in Périgord near Bordeaux, France. His father, Pierre Eyquem, was a Bordeaux merchant and municipal official whose grandfather was the first nobleman of the line. His mother, Antoinette de Louppes (Lopez), was descended from Spanish Jews, called Marranos, who had converted to Catholicism. Montaigne, their third son, was privately tutored and spoke only Latin until the age of six. From 1539 until 1546 he studied at the Collège de Guyenne, in Bordeaux. In 1557 Montaigne obtained the position of councilor in the Bordeaux Parlement (government), where he met his closest friend, Étienne de La Boétie (1530–1563). The two men shared many interests, especially in classical antiquity. La Boétie died from dysentery (an infectious disease causing extreme diarrhea) in 1563. Montaigne was with him through the nine days of his illness. The loss of his friend was a serious emotional blow that Montaigne later described in his essay titled "Of Friendship."

In 1565 Montaigne married Françoise de la Chassaigne, daughter of a co-councilor in the Bordeaux Parlement. They had six daughters, of whom only one survived to adulthood. Montaigne and his wife were apparently compatible, but the marriage was sometimes cool—he believed that marriage ranked somewhat lower than friendship. In "Of Friendship" as quoted in *Selected Essays* translated by Donald M. Frame, Montaigne wrote:

> As for marriage, besides its being a bargain to which only the entrance is free, its continuance being constrained and forced, depending otherwise than on our will, and a bargain ordinarily made for other ends, there supervene [interfere] a thousand foreign tangles to unravel, enough to break the thread and trouble the course of a lively affection; whereas in friendship there are no dealings or business except itself.

Montaigne's father died in 1568, and as a result, Montaigne inherited the rank of lord. Before his death, Pierre Eyquem had persuaded his son to translate into French the *Book of Creatures or Natural Theology* by the fifteenth-century Spanish theologian Raymond of Sabunde (also Sebond; died 1436). The work was an apologia (apology) for the Christian religion based on proof gained from human experience and from the observation of nature. From his work on this translation, which he published in 1569, Montaigne later developed the longest of his many essays, "The Apology for Raymond Sebond." In the essay, Montaigne presented his philosophy of skepticism (attitude of doubt), attacked human knowledge as presumptuous and arrogant, and suggested that one's knowledge of his or her own true self could result only from awareness of ignorance.

Asks "What do I know?"

In 1570 Montaigne resigned from the Bordeaux Parlement and retired to his country estate, where he began writing *Essais* (Essays). Ten years later books one and two were published in Bordeaux. In *Essays* Montaigne used self-portrayal as a method for reaching conclusions about human experience in general. He was not a systematic thinker, however, and he did not maintain a single point of view. Instead, he preferred to show the randomness of his own thought as representative of the self-contradiction to which all people are prone. Montaigne's characteristic motto was "Que sais-je?" ("What do I know?") Although he was skeptical about the power of human reason, he argued that each person should have self-knowledge in order to live happily.

Since Montaigne believed that "each man bears the complete stamp of the human condition," his essays can also be seen as portraits of humankind in all its diversity. He constantly attacked the presumption, arrogance, and pride of human beings, yet he held the highest view of human dignity. As a skeptic, Montaigne opposed intolerance and fanaticism, saying that truth is never one-sided. He championed individual freedom but held that even repressive laws should be obeyed. He feared violence and anarchy (lawlessness or political disorder) and was suspicious of any radical proposals that might jeopardize the existing order. Acceptance and detachment were for him the keys to happiness.

One of Montaigne's best-known essays is "Of Cannibals," in which he contemplated the recently discovered society of cannibals (people who eat other humans) in Brazil in the New World (the European term for the Americas). He concluded that "civilized" people may be no better or worse than "savages." In fact, he concluded that civilization had smothered the natural instincts of human beings. As quoted in *Selected Essays* translated by Donald M. Frame, Montaigne said:

> ... I think there is nothing barbarous and savage in this nation, from what I have been told, except that each man calls barbarism whatever is not his own practice; for indeed it seems we have no other test of truth and reason than the example and pattern of the opinions and customs of the country we live in. *There* is always the perfect religion, the perfect government, the perfect and accomplished usage in all things. Those people are wild, just as we call wild fruits that Nature has produced by herself and in her normal course; whereas really it is those that we have changed artificially and led astray from the common order, that we should rather call wild.... It is not reasonable that art should win the place of honor over our great and powerful mother Nature. We have so overloaded the beau-

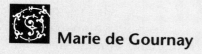

Marie de Gournay

Marie de Gournay (1565–1645) compiled an expanded edition of Montaigne's *Essays* that was published after his death. Gournay met Montaigne in 1588, and they formed an intense pupil-mentor relationship. He became her "second father" and she was his "adoptive daughter." Gournay was devastated when Montaigne died in 1592. She decided to honor his memory with a new edition of *Essays*. Drawing upon his notes, she published the work in 1595. She later issued several other editions. For the first she wrote a highly personal preface (introduction) in which she championed Montaigne as a great genius and herself as an intellectual woman fighting discrimination from men. Gournay thus came across as a strong feminist (one who supports equal rights for women), provoking antifeminist hostility that was directed toward her for the rest of her life. Nevertheless, she struggled—with remarkable success—to maintain a literary salon (discussion group) in Paris.

Although Gournay came from a wealthy family, her father was in financial difficulty when he died in 1577. Marie, therefore, had no income from his estate, and she depended on writing to make a living. In 1594 she published *Le proumenoir de Monsieur de Montaigne* (The promenade of Monsieur Montaigne), a fictional work based on a conversation she had with Montaigne during a stroll. The plot concerned a princess who was destroyed by reckless passion and the betrayal of a man. Gournay also wrote an autobiography, poetry, and feminist essays. Most notable among the essays is *Egalité des homme et des femmes* (Equality of men and women; 1622), which she revised many times. In 1626 she published the first collection of her works, *L'ombre de la Damoiselle de Gournay* (The shadow of Miss de Gournay). Gournay's writings received little attention after her death. In the late twentieth century, however, she began to attract scholarly respect for her literary abilities and her feminist views. By the 1990s a number of new editions and translations of her works were being published.

ty and richness of her works by our inventions that we have quite smothered her. . . .

"Adoptive daughter" edits *Essays*

From 1580 until 1584 Montaigne served as mayor of Bordeaux, and he indirectly defended his regime in the essay "Of Husbanding Your Will." Late in 1580 Montaigne began a fifteen-month trip through Germany, Switzerland, Austria, and Italy. He visited many mineral baths and spas (health resorts) in hopes of finding relief from a chronic kidney stone condition. His journal of these travels, though not intended for publication, was published in 1774. Montaigne was in failing health during his last years, so his "adoptive daughter," Marie de Gournay (see accompanying box), worked on the expanded edition of his works. Drawing mainly from notes made by Montaigne, Gournay published the edition in 1595, three years after his death. It was the basis of the 1603 English-language edition by John Florio, which was a source for Shakespeare's play *Tempest* as well as the works of other playwrights.

For More Information

Books

Montaigne, Michel de. *Selected Essays*. Donald M. Frame, translator. New York: Van Nostrand, 1941.

Web Sites

"Montaigne, Michel de." *Encyclopedia.com*. [Online] Available http://www.encyclopedia.com/searchpool.asp?target=@DOCTITLE%20Montaigne%20%20Michel%20Eyquem%20%20seigneur%20de, April 5, 2002.

"Montaigne, Michel de." *Essays*. [Online] Available http://www.orst.edu/instruct/phl302/texts/montaigne/m-essays_contents.html, April 5, 2002.

Montaigne, Michel de. *"On Cannibals."* [Online] Available http://www.wsu.edu:8080/~wldciv/world_civ_reader/world_civ_reader_2/montaigne.html, April 5, 2002.

Sunshine for Women. *Marie de Gournay, (1565–1645)*. [Online] Available http://www.pinn.net/~sunshine/march99/gournay2.html, April 5, 2002.

Claudio Monteverdi

May 15, 1567
Cremona, Italy
November 29, 1643
Venice, Italy

Composer

C laudio Monteverdi (1567–1643) was the foremost Italian composer of the seventeenth century. During his long career he mastered many forms of music, but he is best known for his operas. Monteverdi was one of the most experimental composers working between 1590 and 1625. During these years he introduced more expressiveness and drama into music, notably through what he called the *stile concitato* (agitated style). As early as 1600, Giovanni Maria Artusi (c. 1545–1613), a well-known music theorist, criticized Monteverdi for engaging in harsh "modernisms." His music represents the transition from the Renaissance into the baroque period (an era in music and the other arts that was characterized by heightened exuberance and drama). Monteverdi now ranks as one of the major European composers of all time.

Experiments with new music form

Monteverdi was born in Cremona, Italy, on May 15, 1567. Historians suggest that his mother, Maddalena, and father, Baldassare, a doctor, were probably musical, for both

Claudio Monteverdi.
Reproduced by permission of Archive Photos, Inc.

Claudio and his brother Giulio Cesare became professional musicians. It is most likely that Monteverdi was a choirboy at the local cathedral (district church) and studied composition (process of composing musical works) with the music director, Marc' Antonio Ingegneri (c. 1547–1592). Little is actually known about Monteverdi's life until 1589, when he tried unsuccessfully to secure a job in Milan. Nevertheless, this was a productive period for him. He published two books of songs, *Madrigali spirituali* (Spritiual madrigals; 1583) and *Canzonette* (Songs; 1584), and his first two books of madrigals, or short vocal pieces based on poems (1587, 1590).

Perhaps in 1590 or the year after, Monteverdi became a string player (one who plays stringed instruments) at the court of Vincenzo Gonzaga (1562–1612), duke of Mantua. He held this position in 1592, the same year he published his third madrigal book. He remained at Mantua for about twenty years. During this time Monteverdi accompanied the duke on two visits to foreign countries. The first, in 1595, was a military expedition to Hungary to fight the Muslim Turks (inhabitants of Turkey who followed the Islam religion), archenemies of European Christians. This experience made a deep impression on Monteverdi. On the second journey, in 1599, they went to Liège, Antwerp, and Brussels, cities in present-day Belgium. Shortly before the second trip Monteverdi married Claudia Cattaneo. They had three children before Claudia's death in 1607.

In 1602 Monteverdi was promoted to *maestro della cappella* (chorus master) at the Gonzaga court. Within the next five years he published two more madrigal books and the first set of compositions called *Scherzi musicali,* a form of vocal chamber music. (Vocal chamber music is composed for singers who perform in a private room or small auditorium, usually with one singer for each part. A part is a separate melody sung along with other, interrelated melodies.) The *Scherzi* were edited by Monteverdi's brother Giulio Cesare, who had previously been appointed to the court of Mantua. In this volume Giulio Cesare explained Monteverdi's views on such musical forms as *prima prattica* and *seconda prattica.* *Prima prattica,* consisting mainly of madrigals for five voices, was the style that dominated music until the late sixteenth century. *Seconda prattica* was a new style in which the text of a poem dictated the character and form of the music. Until

 **Opera**

The term "opera" originated after the Renaissance period to refer to a full-length musical drama with costumes and staging. It is sung entirely throughout with no dialogue (spoken parts). The earliest operas had plots that mixed singing with speaking.

La Dafne is generally considered to be the earliest known opera. The music was composed by Jacopo Peri (1562–1633), and the text was written by Ottavio Rinuccini (1562–1602). It was performed in 1598 Florence, Italy, during Carnival. (Carnival is a festival held before Lent, the Christian observance of forty week days of fasting and prayer between Ash Wednesday and Easter Sunday.) *La Dafne* was originally planned and sponsored by the Florentine silk merchant Jacopo Corsi (1561–1602). Only six short fragments of music have survived from this work. Peri and Rinuccini collaborated on a second opera, *L'Euridice*, which was first performed in Florence in 1600. This is thought to be the first surviving opera.

The plots and characters of *La Dafne, L'Euridice,* and several other early operas revolve around heroes of ancient mythology (stories about gods, goddesses, and legendary figures). These heroes find their salvation through prowess in or support of the arts. This theme reflected the determination of the nobility in Florence to transform their city into a cultural center like ancient Athens, Greece. Moreover, they wanted to show that their own patronage was crucial to the return of the arts and learning of antiquity, which was considered the golden age of human achievement. The musical style and dramatic form of operas also paralleled or imitated those of antiquity.

1605 Monteverdi's musical compositions were in the *prima prattica* tradition. Thereafter he experimented with *seconda practtica*, composing pieces for various combinations of voices and instruments.

Composes first operas

In 1607 Monteverdi published his first opera, *La favola d'Orfeo,* which was performed in Mantua. Opera was not a new musical form (see accompanying box), but this work was notable for combining many popular elements and introducing new concepts. *Orfeo* tells the story of the Greek god Orpheus who makes a journey to Hades (the underworld) to rescue his wife Euridyce. Orpheus plays his lyre (an early form of the harp) and charms Pluto, the Greek god of the underworld, who had abducted Euridyce. The opera represented a cross section of musical forms of the early seventeenth century—including choruses in complex harmony (several interrelated melodies sung at the same time), solo ensembles (small groups of singers), arias (elaborate melodies performed by one singer), dances, and independent instrumental pieces. The orchestra consisted of more than forty kinds of instruments, including harpsichords (type of piano), organs, strings, woodwinds (reed instruments), and brass (horns such as trumpets and trombones). The music director mainly decided which instruments played when, though in certain instances Monteverdi specified the instrumentation. For example, the spirits of Hades are accompanied by two organs, five trombones, two bass gambas, and a violone. The combination of these instruments produces a strikingly dark sound. In fact, as a result of *Orfeo* trombones have traditionally been associated with anything "infernal" (pertaining to the underworld or hell).

Orfeo was revived frequently during Monteverdi's lifetime. One of his other operas, *Arianna,* was even more popular. The celebrated lament (song of sorrow), *Lasciatemi morire,* is the only fragment to have survived from *Arianna.* Arranged for five voices and included in Monteverdi's sixth madrigal book, it set a fashion for nearly every opera for the next one hundred fifty years or so. In 1610 Monteverdi published another of his finest sacred works, the highly complex *Vespers,* which combined old and new musical forms for choirs, soloists, and several instruments.

Moves to Venice

Vincenzo Gonzaga died in 1612, and Monteverdi was dismissed from his position by the duke's successor, Ferdinand. For more than a year Monteverdi tried to find employment that would match his fame as a composer. Finally, in 1613, he was appointed to one of the most prestigious musical positions in Italy, that of *maestro di cappella* at the famous basilica (church) of Saint Mark's in Venice. Monteverdi spent the rest of his life in Venice. In 1627 his son Massimiliano was arrested by the Inquisition (a church court set up to find and punish heretics, or those who violate the laws of the church) and found not guilty the following year. Around 1632 Monteverdi entered the priesthood.

Monteverdi had a productive career during his thirty years at Saint Mark's. In addition to completely reorganizing the whole musical setup and raising the standards of the singers and instrumentalists, he composed a quantity of sacred and secular (nonreligious) music. Most of the sacred music consisted of masses (music performed during the Catholic communion service), although he composed songs, litanies (repetitive chants), and Magnificats (musical settings of the canticle, or song, of Mary in the biblical book of Luke). Monteverdi's secular music can be divided into chamber and dramatic. The chamber category included madrigals and the second set of *Scherzi musicali* (1632). The dramatic category included nine operas, three ballets (dances with poses and steps combined with leaps and turns), and the dramatic cantata (compositions for one or more voices and instruments) *Il combattimento di Tancredi e Clorinda* (1624). This work is still performed today, as are the ballets *Tirisi e Clori* (1616) and *Volgendo il ciel* (1637). Monteverdi's last two operas, *Il ritorno d'Ulisse in patria* (The return of Ulysses to his native country; 1641) and *L'incoronazione di Poppea* (The coronation of Poppea; 1642), have also survived. *Poppea* is now considered one of the masterpieces of European music.

Music showcases drama

Poppea was the first opera on an historical subject (as opposed to mythological, biblical, or poetical subjects). It is based on the true story of the Roman emperor Nero (A.D. 37–68) and his love affair with Poppea Sabina (died A.D. 65), a beautiful court prostitute (a woman whose official function was to be available for sexual relations with noblemen at court). Nero's obsession led him to repudiate, or reject, the rightful empress of Rome, his wife Ottavia, and to crown Poppea as the true empress. This ill-fated union ended in Poppea's murder at the hands of Nero. (According to one account, Nero kicked or stomped Poppea to death.) Monteverdi's opera, however, deals only with Nero's early obsession, his repudiation of Ottavia, and the coronation of

Poppea. In composing *The Coronation of Poppea* Monteverdi largely rejected spectacular effects and relied more on characterization of the leading figures. He balanced music and drama, making the music seem to spring directly from the actions of the characters.

Monteverdi's influence, both before and after his death, was not equal to his achievement. He had no real followers who would have promoted his musical style. One reason was that musical taste and fashion were changing rapidly during the last phase of the Renaissance and the beginning of the baroque period. Nevertheless, today Monteverdi is regarded as one of the outstanding composers of all time. He used music as a vehicle for drama, portraying a wide range of human emotions and personalities.

Singers perform Claudio Monteverdi's *The Coronation of Poppea*. In composing this work Monteverdi largely rejected spectacular effects and relied more on the characterization of leading figures. *©Robbbie Jack/Corbis. Reproduced by permission of Corbis Corporation.*

For More Information

Books

Kiel, Dyke, and Gary K. Adams. *Claudio Monteverdi: A Guide to Research.* New York: Garland Publishing, Inc., 1989.

Web Sites

"Monteverdi, Claudio." *Essentials of Music.* [Online] Available http://www.essentialsofmusic.com/composer/monteverdi.html, April 5, 2002.

Monteverdi, Claudio—Innovator and Madrigalist. [Online] Available http://web.azstarnet.com/public/packages/reelbook/153-4028.htm, April 5, 2002.

"Monteverdi, Claudio." *Unitel—"L'Orfeo.* [Online] Available http://www.unitel.classicalmusic.com/classica/112200.htm, April 5, 2002.

National Public Radio. "Monteverdi, Claudio." *Milestones of the Millenium.* [Online] Available http://npr.org/programs/specials/milestones/990519.motm.monteverdi.html, April 5, 2002.

Thomas More

February 6, 1478
London, England
July 6, 1535
London, England

Humanist, author, statesman

The life of the English humanist and statesman Thomas More exemplifies the political and spiritual upheaval of the Protestant Reformation, the movement to reform the Catholic Church. Now known for his revolutionary work *Utopia*, More was beheaded for opposing the religious policy of **Henry VIII** (1491–1547; see entry).

Influenced by humanists

Thomas More was born in London on February 6, 1478, to parents whose families were connected with the city's legal community. His education began at a prominent London school, Saint Anthony's. In 1490 he went to work for Archbishop John Morton (c. 1420–1500), the closest adviser of King Henry VII (1457–1509; reigned 1485–1509). In 1492 he attended Oxford University in England, where he first encountered Greek studies. There he seems to have been tempted to become a priest or a monk. Following his father's lead, however, More began studying law when he returned to London two years later. By 1498 More had gained membership in

"This means that if they suddenly had to part with all the gold and silver they possess—a fate which in any other country would be thought equivalent to having one's guts torn out—nobody in Utopia would care two hoots."

Thomas More in Utopia.

Thomas More.
Photograph courtesy of The Library Congress.

253

Lincoln's Inn, an influential lawyers' fraternity. Around this time More also came under the influence of John Colet (c. 1466–1519), an important scholar and preacher.

Colet was educated in Italy and brought back to England a controversial method of studying Scriptures (text of the Bible, the Christian holy book), which was developed by humanists. Humanists were scholars devoted to reviving the literary and philosophical works of ancient Greek and Roman writers. They believed that Scriptures should be read within an historical context instead of being regarded as sacred texts that should never be questioned or analyzed. Colet caused a sensation by lecturing on the historical aspects of Paul's Epistles (Letters) to the Romans from the New Testament (the second half of the Bible). Around 1498 More similarly drew attention to himself by lecturing on *City of God* by Saint Augustine of Hippo (354–430), one of the first Christian theologians.

In 1499 More met the famous Dutch humanist **Erasmus Desiderius** (c. 1466–1536; see entry) and began studying Greek. Together More and Erasmus collaborated on translating works by the Greek satirist Lucian of Samosata (c.120–c.190). Lucian had parodied, or made fun of, pagan superstitions and was widely regarded as an atheist (one who does not believe in God or gods). More and Erasmus learned from Lucian the art of humorous ridicule for a serious purpose, aiming at criticizing the superstitions and immoral practices of Christians without directly doing so. At the time, questioning church doctrines and superstitions was very dangerous. Using parody or satire was a way to disguise one's true message while calling church traditions into question.

Develops political views

While More continued his studies and translations with Erasmus, he advanced in his career and took on family responsibilities. In 1504 or 1505 he married Jane Colt, a young woman from the country. After bearing four children she died in 1511. Within a month More was married again, to a widow named Alice Middleton.

When King Henry VII died in 1509, More greeted his death with passionate poems dedicated to young Henry VIII. More was sharply critical of the old king, making Henry VII

English statesman and scholar Thomas More surrounded by his family. *Reproduced by permission of Hulton Archive.*

seem a mean and overbearing ruler. In one of these poems, which were published in a collection in 1518, More expressed his preference for a republic (government consisting of representatives of the people) over a monarchy (government controlled by one ruler). Senators in a republic, he said, are chosen by reasoned argument, but monarchs are chosen by chance. He recognized, however, that people rarely had any choice in the government that rules them. In twelve of his poems he condemned tyranny, or rule by extreme force that limits the rights and freedoms of citizens. Also during this time More undertook a history of King Richard III (1452–1483; ruled 1483–85), but he may have given up writing this work to devote his time to *Utopia*.

Publishes *Utopia*

In 1511 More was appointed undersheriff of London. This job involved acting as an adviser at the court of King

Henry VIII and as a negotiator with foreign merchants. Four years later More took his first official trip abroad, to Antwerp in present-day Belgium. When he returned to London he began *Utopia,* a fiction that he wrote in Latin and modeled on the ancient Greek philosopher Plato's *Republic.* Published in 1516, *Utopia* describes an imaginary land that is free of the ostentation, greed, and violence that plagued the society of Henry's England. More's inspiration for the book was the discovery of the Americas.

In the first part of *Utopia* More recounts his meeting with a sunburned Portuguese mariner named Raphael Hythloday, who has been with the explorer Amerigo Vespucci (1454–1512) in the New World. Hythloday is a philosophical traveler, both opinionated and virtuous. As Hythloday, More, and More's friend Peter Giles converse, Hythloday launches into a critique of the ills of European society. Every place he has seen in his voyages seems superior to Europe. He bitterly criticizes the injustice of the English legal system that allows a few to amass great wealth, while multitudes endure such extreme poverty that they have to beg or steal to survive.

In the second part of *Utopia* Hythloday speaks enthusiastically of a republic on an island off the coast of Brazil. It had been founded 1,760 years earlier by a compassionate conqueror named Utopus, who wrote a constitution for a system that would make its citizens virtuous and its society secure. Hythloday then goes on to describe in great detail the structure of this society. The root of all social problems can be traced to the holding of private property. A person who has property develops pride and wants to acquire more wealth, oftentimes at the expense of others who have little or nothing. In the Utopian society, personal property, private life, and individuality are abolished, and those who break the laws are punished by enslavement or death. Gold, silver, and jewels are made essentially worthless (see accompanying box). Husbands and wives are alone only when they sleep. Utopians eat, work, travel, and spend their leisure time in groups. Regulations are severe, and the punishment given for the offenses is central not only to the government, but to religion as well. All Utopians are required to believe that God exists and that in a future life he will reward good and punish evil deeds done in this life. Without such a belief, no one can be a good citizen. The punishment of human law must be backed up by the threat of

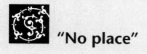

"No place"

Thomas More believed that personal property is the basis of all social problems. Nevertheless, he knew that even when personal property has been eliminated, the desire for wealth remains. More addressed this issue in Book Two of *Utopia*. In the following passage Hythloday, the main character, explains how gold and jewels have been made essentially worthless in Utopia and why that society works so well.

According to this system [of government], plates and drinking- vessels, though beautifully designed, are made of quite cheap stuff like glass or earthenware. But silver and gold are the normal materials, in private houses as well as communal dining-halls, for the humblest items of domestic equipment, such as chamber-pots [toilets]. They also use chains and fetters [chains for the feet] of solid gold to immobilize slaves, and anyone who commits a really shameful crime is forced to go about with gold rings on his ears and fingers, a gold necklace round his neck, and a crown

of gold on his head. In fact, they do everything they can to bring these materials into contempt [disregard]. This means that if they suddenly had to part with all the gold and silver they possess—a fate which in any other country would be thought equivalent to having one's guts torn out—nobody in Utopia would care two hoots.

It's much the same with jewels. There are pearls to be found on the beaches, diamonds and garnets on certain types of rock—but they never bother to look for them. However, if they happen to come across one, they pick it up and polish it for some toddler to wear. At first, children are terribly proud of such jewellry—until they're old enough to register that it's only worn in the nursery. Then, without any prompting from their parents, but purely as a matter of self-respect, they give it up—just as our children grow out of things like dolls, and conkers [a game played by children during the Renaissance], and lucky charms.

Source: More, Thomas. Utopia. Paul Turner, editor. New York: Penguin Books, 1965, pp. 86–87.

divine vengeance. The citizens of Utopia, therefore, readily convert to Christianity. By the end of the book, More had drawn a bleak estimate of the human condition.

Named lord chancellor

In the meantime, Henry VIII had invited More to become a councilor in the royal court. More's deep suspicion of rulers and politics made him reluctant to accept the invitation, but he finally agreed to the appointment in 1517. He went on to build a career in diplomacy, legal service, and finance. More eventually learned that his early doubts about serving Henry had been justified. By 1523 More had risen to the position of speaker of the House of Commons (lower branch of Parliament). Under the direction of the lord chancellor of England, Cardinal Thomas Wolsey (c. 1475–1530), More had to promote a highly unpopular war levy (tax) that was ultimately discontinued. In negotiations with other European countries, More was constantly frustrated by Henry's warlike nature and Wolsey's political ambition. More wanted to stop wars so that the Christian faith and culture could be preserved. In 1529 Henry appointed More lord chancellor of England, replacing Wolsey, who had failed to obtain the pope's approval of the annulment (an order that declares a marriage invalid) of the king's marriage to Catherine of Aragon (1485–1536). More now occupied the highest administrative office in the land. Yet he soon found himself in a distressing role as Henry's chief agent in dealing with the pope.

While serving as chancellor, More was deeply engaged in writings against Lutherans (followers of religious reformer **Martin Luther;** see entry) In such works as *Dialogue Cernynge Heresyes* (1529) and *Apologye* (1533) he defended the Catholic Church, even though he was aware of its flaws. More steadfastly held that heretics (those who violate the laws of the church) should be burned for their blasphemy (showing of contempt) against God's true church. At the same time, Henry was drawing further away from the church because the pope still refused to grant him a divorce. In 1532 More resigned from office, primarily because of illness and distress over Henry's outright threat to break from the church. Finally, Henry simply announced that the pope had no authority in England. Statutes passed by the Reformation Parliament in 1533 and 1534 named the king supreme head of the church, now called the Anglican Church or Church of England, and cut all ties with the papacy. The Anglican Church thus became an independent national body.

More recognized the dangers posed by his pro-Catholic writings, so he tried to avoid political controversy. But Henry pressured him to reject the pope's jurisdiction in England. More refused Henry's order because he did not want to contribute to disharmony within the Christian world. In April 1534 More was summoned for interrogation by royal officials. When he did not change his position he was put on trial for treason (betrayal of one's country) and found guilty.

He was beheaded on July 6, 1535. Although More is most often remembered as the man who defied Henry VIII, the significance of his life extends beyond the realm of English history. During the turbulent years of the early Reformation, he worked to revitalize Christianity within the church through his active involvement in humanism. In 1935 he was declared a saint by the Catholic Church. More's *Utopia* continues to be read, and is considered a classic work on the ideal society.

For More Information

Books

Ackroyd, Peter. *The Life of Thomas More.* New York: Nan A. Talese, 1998.

More, Thomas. *Utopia.* Paul Turner, editor. New York: Penguin Books, 1965.

Video Recordings

A Man for All Seasons. Burbank, Calif.: RCA/Columbia Pictures Home Video, 1985.

Web Sites

Jokinen, Anniina. "More, Thomas." *The Lumninarium.* [Online] Available http://www.luminarium.org/renlit/tmore.htm, April 5, 2002.

Knight, Kevin. "More, Thomas." *Catholic Encyclopedia.* [Online] Available http://www.newadvent.org/cathen/14689c.htm, April 5, 2002.

"More, Thomas." *Redefining the Sacred.* [Online] Available http://www.folger.edu/institute/sacred/image8.html, April 5, 2002.

Isotta Nogarola

1418
Verona, Italy
1466
Verona, Italy

Writer, scholar

The Italian writer Isotta Nogarola is considered the first woman to become a major figure in the humanist movement. Humanism began in Florence, Italy, in the mid-1300s among scholars who promoted the study of the literary masterpieces of ancient Greece and Rome. They believed that this body of learning, called *studia humanitatis* (humanistic studies), could bring about a cultural rebirth, or renaissance. They also studied the Bible (the Christian holy book) and the works of early Christian thinkers. Humanists had faith in the human potential for great achievements, an idea that was entirely new for the time. They are credited with starting the Renaissance, which spread throughout Italy and northern Europe in the fifteenth century. Nogarola was an active participant in humanist circles. She produced a number of works and conducted extensive correspondence with the important thinkers of her day. She is most famous for "On the Equal and Unequal Sin of Eve and Adam," in which she asserted that Eve (the first woman on Earth, according to biblical tradition) should not bear the responsibility for committing original sin (the concept that all humans are born with a sinful nature).

Retreats to "book-lined cell"

Isotta Nogarola was born into a literary family in Verona, Italy. She received a humanist education along with her older sister Ginevra. While they were teenagers both girls won the attention of northern Italian humanists and courtiers (members of the court). With these learned men they exchanged books and letters that showed their classical training and lively intelligence. In 1438 Ginevra married and ceased her involvement in the discussions of humanist ideas. Isotta continued to participate until 1441, when she became discouraged by attacks on her character. Historians believe these attacks came from men who did not approve of learned women. Isotta Nogarola withdrew from humanist circles to join her mother in her brother's house. She lived, as she put it, in a "book-lined cell" where, like medieval holy women, she continued her studies in solitude.

Nogarola's works fall into two groups, before and after her retirement. In the earlier period, from about 1434 to 1441, she composed an extensive letterbook. It contained her own letters to humanist friends and relatives along with some of their responses. These letters demonstrate Nogarola's knowledge of early Christian and classical authors, as well as her awareness of current political events and the historical tradition of heroic women. The letters also show that she had close relationships with the intellectual and political leaders of northern Italy. Many of the people who corresponded with Nogarola showered her with praise, suggesting that her exceptional achievements were widely known.

The chorus of praise from learned correspondents continued in the second, longer period of Nogarola's life, from about 1441 to 1466. She received tributes from such eminent figures as Ermolao Barbaro the Elder, the bishop (district church official) of Verona. Of special interest are letters from top humanists in Venice, Lauro Quirini and Ludovico Foscarini. Quirini's letter outlined a program of study that urged Nogarola to reach beyond literature written in Latin to read philosophical works in the original Greek. Quirini argued that philosophy (the search for an understanding of reality through speculation) is superior to rhetoric (the art of effective speaking and writing). He suggested that a learned woman had the capacity to master the difficulties of philosophy.

Cassandra Fedele

Cassandra Fedele (1465–1558) was an important Italian woman humanist in the generation after Isotta Nogarola. Although Fedele was active in humanist circles and was one of the most acclaimed women of the time, she accepted the traditional view of women. She believed in the "natural" inferiority of the female sex, and she routinely presented herself as being less important than men. Fedele was born in Venice and received a classical education through the efforts of her father, Angelo Fedele. When Cassandra was a young teenager Angelo represented her as a child prodigy (an exceptionally talented young person). She delivered orations, or formal speeches, standing before the assembled faculty at the University of Padua, the Venetian Senate, and the doge (duke of Venice) himself.

Fedele's first book was published when she was twenty-two, and before she reached the age of thirty, lists of her works were featured in encyclopedias of famous men and women. Her main professional achievement was the letters, perhaps thousands of them, that she exchanged with some of the most celebrated men and women of the day. Fedele never held an academic appointment, but she corresponded with Niccolò Leonico Tomei, a scholar at the University of Padua, and she met regularly with prominent humanists at Padua. Fedele came close to accepting an academic appointment with the Spanish monarchs Isabella I and Ferdinand II. For eight years Fedele corresponded with the queen and her representatives, but she canceled her plans in 1495 after the outbreak of the Italian Wars (1494–1559; a conflict between France and Spain over control of Italy).

Fedele married in 1498 and was widowed in 1520. Childless and almost penniless, she shared cramped quarters with her sister's family until 1547, when Pope Paul III responded to her plea for assistance. He secured an appointment for her as prioress (supervisor) at the orphanage of San Domenico di Castello. In 1556 Fedele made her last public appearance when she delivered an oration welcoming the queen of Poland to Venice. Only two of her published writings survive. One is the small volume she wrote as a girl and the other is *Casandrae Fidelis epistolae et orationes* (Letters and orations of Cassandra Fedele; 1636), which contains 123 letters and 3 orations.

Writes famous dialogue

Perhaps the most famous of Nogarola's letter exchanges was with Foscarini, a Venetian statesman and governor of Verona. In 1451 Nogarola composed a dialogue (written work in the form of a conversation) titled "On the Equal and

Isotta Nogarola's most famous dialogue, "On the Equal and Unequal Sin of Eve and Adam," explored the question of whether Adam or Eve had committed the greater sin in the Garden of Eden.
Reproduced by permission of Hulton Archive.

Unequal Sin of Eve and Adam," which was addressed to Foscarini. In the dialogue she explored the question of whether Adam or Eve committed the greater sin in the Garden of Eden. According to the story in the book of Genesis in the Old Testament (the first part of the Bible), Adam and Eve were the first two people on Earth. They lived in the Garden of Eden, and they had no awareness of evil because they had been forbidden by God to eat apples from the tree of knowledge. One day an evil serpent appeared in the tree and tempted Adam and Eve to eat an apple. Eve took a bite and then persuaded Adam to do the same. God later expelled them from the garden for committing the first sin. This story was used by Christian leaders to prove that because of Eve (woman) all humans are born with original sin—that is, sin is a part of human nature at birth—because she had tempted Adam (man) into an awareness of evil.

On the question of who had committed the greater sin, Foscarini took Adam's side, presenting the traditional argument for Eve's guilt. He pointed out that Eve's moral weakness, not the serpent (evil), was the temptation that made Adam surrender to a sinful act. Nogarola defended Eve, saying that Eve was incapable of choosing between good and evil and therefore should not be held accountable. In one part of the letter that is quoted in *Her Immaculate Hand: Selected Works By and About the Women Humanists of Quattrocento Italy* edited and translated by Margaret L. King and Albert Rabil, Nogarola wrote:

Nostradamus left home to study in Avignon, the religious and academic center of Provence. In class, he sometimes voiced opposition to the teachings of the Catholic priests, who dismissed the study of astrology—the study of how events on Earth are influenced by the positions and movements of the Sun, Moon, planets, and stars—(see accompanying box) and the theories of the Polish astronomer **Nicolaus Copernicus** (1473–1543; see entry). Copernicus had recently gained fame with his theory that the Earth and other planets revolved around the Sun—contrary to the Christian belief that the Earth was the center of the universe. Nostradamus's family warned him to hold his tongue, since he could be easily singled out for persecution because of his Jewish background in the anti-Jewish society of France. Earlier, from his grandfathers he had secretly learned some mystical (spiritual perception of reality that does not rely on the senses) areas of Jewish wisdom, including the Kabbalah (a variety of religious literatures) and alchemy (a science devoted to turning common metals into gold and silver).

In 1525 Nostradamus graduated from the University of Montpellier, where he had studied both medicine and astrology. During the first several years of his career as a doctor he traveled to towns and villages where people were dying of the bubonic plague, an epidemic, or widespread, disease that swept Europe in the fifteenth and sixteenth centuries. Called the "Black Death" because of the festering black sores it left on victims' bodies, the deadly epidemic had no cure. Doctors commonly "bled," or drew large quantities of "diseased" blood from their patients, and knew nothing of how to prevent further infection. They did not realize that unsanitary conditions contributed to the spread of the disease. Nostradamus would prescribe fresh air and water, a low-fat diet, and new bedding for the afflicted. He often administered a remedy made from rosehips (fruit of roses), later discovered to be rich in vitamin C. Entire towns recovered with these herbal remedies, which were common at the time, but Nostradamus's beliefs about infection control could have resulted in charges of heresy (violation of church laws) and a sentence of death.

Begins foretelling future

Word of Nostradamus's healing powers made him a celebrated figure in Provence. He wrote a book listing the doctors

Astrology

Astrology was considered a science during the early Renaissance period. Closely related to astronomy, astrology is the study of how events on Earth are influenced by the positions and movements of the Sun, Moon, planets, and stars. Astrologers believe that the position of heavenly bodies at the exact moment of a person's birth reflect his or her character. Later movements of heavenly bodies determine that person's destiny.

Historians estimate that the earliest known form of astrology was practiced by the Chaldeans, who lived in Babylonia (now Iraq), in 3000 B.C. Astrology was also part of ancient cultures in China and India, and evidence of astrological practices has been found in Maya ruins in Central America. Astrology reached Greece by the fifth century B.C., and Greek philosophers such as Pythagoras and Plato incorporated it into their study of religion and astronomy. Astrology was popular in Europe throughout the Middle Ages, although it had been condemned by church leaders since the early days of Christianity. Like alchemy, astrology eventually fell out of favor when scientists discovered new facts about the Earth and the universe. Nevertheless, astrology enjoyed considerable popularity during the Renaissance. Monarchs and noblemen had astrologers such as Nostradamus create charts called horoscopes, which mapped the position of astronomical bodies at certain times and were used to predict future events.

and pharmacists (people who prepare medicines) he had met in southern Europe. He also translated anatomical texts (studies of the human body) and developed recipes for gourmet foods. Nostradamus received his doctorate from Montpellier in 1529. He taught at the university for three years, but left when his radical ideas about disease were censured, or officially reprimanded. He chose a wife from among the many offered to him by wealthy and connected families, and settled in the town of Agen. Then the plague killed his wife and two young children. Because the famed physician could not save his own family, citizens suddenly looked upon him with scorn. His in-laws sued for the return of the dowry (money or property provided by a bride's family) given to him. His patron, a scholar and philosopher named Julius Caesar Scaliger (1484–1558), also broke ties with him. A chance remark Nostradamus had once made about a statue of Mary (mother of Jesus of Nazareth, the founder of Christianity) landed him in court defending himself against charges of heresy. He fled the area when he was told to appear before the feared Inquisition, a church court set up to search out and punish heretics.

For the next several years Nostradamus traveled through southern Europe. Modern scholars suggest that this difficult period probably awakened his powers of clairvoyance, or ability to predict the future. By 1544 torrential rains were bringing more disaster to southern France, which had already been devastated by the plague (a series of disease epidemics). Nostradamus appeared in Marseilles and then in Aix, where he managed to halt the spread of disease and was again celebrated for his skills. Moving to the town of Salon, he set up a medical practice, remarried, and began a new family. Although he was outwardly a practicing Catholic, he secretly spent the night hours in his study meditating over his brass bowl. The meditation would put him into a trance. Scholars theorize that he may have used herbs to achieve such a state. In these trances Nostradamus would have visions about events that were to happen during the coming year.

Predicts king's death

Nostradamus wrote down his visions, and in 1550 he began publishing them in *Centuries,* (also called *Almanacs* and *Prophesies*) which appeared annually for the next fifteen years. In the *Almanacs* Nostradamus described astrological phases for the next year and he offered hints of upcoming events in rhymed four-line verses called quatrains. The *Almanacs* became immensely popular, and soon Nostradamus was even more famous in France. By now his visions were such an integral part of his scholarship that he decided to channel them into one massive work for future generations. He would call this book *Centuries*. Each of the ten planned volumes would contain one hundred predictions in quatrain (four lines of verse) form, and the next two thousand years of humanity would be forecasted.

Nostradamus began working on *Centuries* in 1554. The first seven volumes were published in Lyon the following year and made him a celebrated figure. His writings attracted the interest of France's royal family. In 1556 he was invited to the Paris court King Henry II (1519–1559; ruled 1547–59) and the queen, **Catherine de Médicis** (1519–1589; see entry). Catherine belonged to the powerful Medici family of Florence, Italy, who were known for their political ambitions. She hoped that Nostradamus could give her guidance regarding the futures of her seven children, for whom he cast horoscopes (see accompanying box). Nostradamus had also been summoned to explain Quatrain 35 of *Centuries I*, which apparently referred to Henry. It read: "The young lion will overcome the older one/ On the field of combat in single battle/ He will pierce his eyes through a golden cage/ Two wounds made one, then he dies a cruel death."

Nostradamus told the king to avoid any ceremonial jousting (a contest between two people with lances riding on horses) during his forty-first year (1559), a warning that had also been given by Henry's own astrologer. Nostradamus spent the next three years ensconced, or sheltered, in the luxury of the royal court. He drew up astrology charts for four of the royal couple's sons and predicted that they all would become kings. Then Nostradamus received word that Catholic authorities were again becoming suspicious of his soothsaying (foretelling future events) and were about to investigate him. He returned to his wife and children in Salon. After completing volumes eight through ten of *Centuries*, Nostradamus began work on two additional volumes. (He would not allow volumes eight through ten to be published until after his death.) On June 28, 1559—in his forty-first year—King Henry was injured in a jousting tournament. With thousands watching, his opponent's lance penetrated the visor of his helmet and lodged in his brain. The blinded king died ten days later.

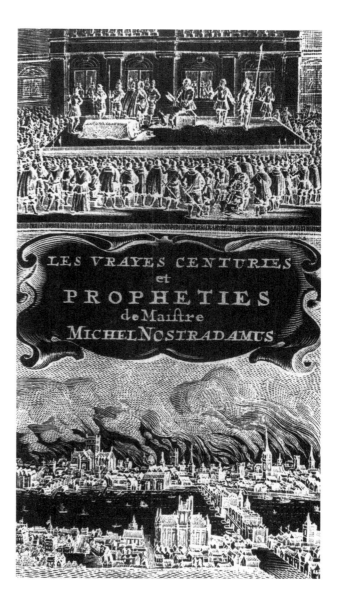

The original title page from Nostradamus's book *Centuries*. ©*Bettmann/Corbis. Reproduced by permission of Corbis Corporation.*

Horoscope

A horoscope is a diagram in the shape of a circle, called the ecliptic, which represents the Earth's orbit in its annual rotation around the Sun. The ecliptic is divided into twelve sections known as the signs of the Zodiac, and each sign is associated with a set of human characteristics. The twelve signs are Aries, Taurus, Gemini, Cancer, Leo, Virgo, Libra, Scorpio, Sagittarius, Capricorn, Aquarius, and Pisces. Each planet, including the Sun and the Moon, is associated with basic human drives. The ecliptic is also divided into twelve houses corresponding to the twenty-four-hour period during which the Earth rotates once on its axis. Each house is related to certain aspects of a person's life.

In casting a horoscope, an astrologer chooses a date in the future and then assigns each planet a particular sign according to where the planet appears on the ecliptic for that time. The astrologer then makes a prediction about events that will take place by interpreting the position of the planets within the signs and the houses. Astrologers also give a person a certain sign, such as an Aquarius or a Taurus, according to the sign occupied by the Sun at the time of the person's birth. It is called the person's Sun sign.

Although astrology fell out of favor in the sixteenth century because of new theories of the universe, it remains popular today. Most newspapers and magazines feature horoscope sections that are avidly consulted by readers. In 2000 the Kepler College of Astrological Arts and Sciences was founded in Seattle, Washington. The school offers bachelor and master's degrees in astrology.

Predicted twentieth-century events?

Already a celebrity in France, Nostradamus became a figure inspiring both awe and fright among the populace. His other prophecies regarding France's royal line were consulted, and most seemed to predict only death and tragedy. Catherine de Médicis visited Nostradamus in Salon during her royal tour of 1564, and he again told her that all four of her sons would become kings. This prediction came true, but the children met dismal ends: one son became king of Poland, but was murdered by a priest; another died before carrying out a plot to kill another brother; two died young as well; the three daughters also met tragic fates. The family's House of Valois came to an end with the death of one of the daughters, Queen Margaret (1553–1615), wife of King Henry IV (Henry of Navarre; 1553–1610; ruled 1572–89).

Nostradamus himself died in 1566, after many years of suffering from gout (a disease that causes painful swelling of the body). Naturally, he predicted his own end, although records show that he was off by a year. Many translations of his *Centuries* and treatises on their significance appeared in the generations following his death. For the next two hundred years the Vatican (office of the pope) issued the Index of Forbidden Books. *Centuries* was always on the list. *Centuries* remains popular to the present day, and interpreters claim Nostradamus predicted many important twentieth-century events. For instance, he reportedly warned that the German Nazi leader Adolf Hitler (1889–1945) would rise to power in the 1930s. Another of Nostradamus's supposed predictions was the explosion of the U.S. space shuttle *Challenger* in 1986.

For More Information

Books

Fontbrune, Jean-Charles de. *Nostradamus 2: Into the Twenty-first Century*. Alexis Lykiard, translator. New York: Holt, Rinehart, and Winston, 1985.

Web Sites

"How Nostradamus Works." *How Stuff Works*. [Online] Available http://www.howstuffworks.com/nostradamus.htm, April 5, 2002.

"Nostradamus." *MSN Encarta*. [Online] Available http://encarta.msn.com/find/Concise.asp?z=1&pg=2&ti=761568156, April 5, 2002.

Nostradamus Repository. [Online] Available http://www.nostradamus-repository.org/, April 5, 2002.

Giovanni Pierluigi da Palestrina

December 27, 1525
Palestrina, Italy
February 2, 1594
Rome, Italy

Composer

The Italian musician Giovanni Pierluigi da Palestrina was the foremost composer of the sixteenth century. His sacred works represent one of the great achievements of Renaissance music. The Renaissance was a cultural movement which began in Italy in the mid-1300s. It was initiated by scholars called humanists who promoted the human-centered values of ancient Greece and Rome. Humanist ideals were soon influencing the arts, literature, philosophy, science, religion, and politics in Italy.

Begins as choir master

Born Giovanni Pierluigi, the composer adopted the name of his native town, Palestrina, which is located near Rome. Little is known about his early life, though it is assumed that at the age of seven he was a choir singer at the church of Saint Agapit in Palestrina. Records show that he was a member of the choir at the basilica (church) of Santa Maria Maggiore in Rome in 1537. Palestrina served at the basilica until his nineteenth birthday. During this time he

probably received musical training from Jacques Arcadelt (c. 1505–1568). In 1544 Palestrina returned to his native town as organist and singing master at the local church. During the next six years he married, fathered the first of his three sons, and began composing. Most important for his future career was the attention given his music by the new bishop of Palestrina, Giovanni del Monte (1487–1555). Del Monte became Pope Julius III in 1550 (reigned 1550–55), and the following year he appointed Palestrina choirmaster of the Julian Chapel at Saint Peter's Basilica in Rome.

All singers in this choir traditionally were unmarried, and they were admitted only after rigorous examination. Since the pope had ignored these requirements, Palestrina's appointment was viewed with little enthusiasm. In 1554 Palestrina published his first book of masses (music that accompanies the Catholic communion service) and dedicated it to Julius. The following year he was promoted to singer in the pope's choir. When Julius died the following year, Pope Paul

Giovanni Pierluigi da Palestrina | 273

IV (1476–1559; reigned 1555–59) enforced the celibacy rule (the requirement that musicians be unmarried) as part of the Catholic Reformation (a reform movement within the Roman Catholic Church) and dismissed Palestrina from Julian Chapel. The pope then appointed Palestrina choirmaster at the Basilica of Saint John Lateran, where he remained until 1560. For the next six years Palestrina held posts at various other churches. From 1566 to 1570 he was music director for Cardinal Ippolito II d'Este (1509–1572), an outstanding patron of the arts. In 1571 Palestrina was reappointed choirmaster at the Julian Chapel. Seven years later he was given the title of master of music at Saint Peter's, a position he held for the rest of his life.

Known as "Prince of Music"

Palestrina's works included the major types of late Renaissance music: masses, motets (vocal works based on sacred texts, sometimes accompanied by instruments), and madrigals (short vocal works based on poems). He wrote 105 masses and 250 motets, but madrigals played a small role in his compositions because he was primarily interested in sacred music. Using original techniques, he frequently adapted polyphony (two or more melodies forming harmony) to such traditional forms as plainsong (early Christian chants), hymns, and biblical texts. He often created as many as eight interwoven parts in counterpoint, or separate melodies sung above or below a main melody. Yet Palestrina had a carefully controlled, sensitive style that adhered closely to his chosen text and lacked the drama of music by other composers at the time. His religious compositions, especially the masses, were of such high quality that he was called the "Prince of Music." Palestrina's most famous mass was *Missa Papae Marcelli,* which he dedicated to Pope Marcellus II (1501–1555; reigned 1555) in 1555.

Palestrina is also known as the creator of the oratorio. It is a lengthy religious choral work that features recitatives (singing that resembles speaking), arias (vocal solos), and choruses without action or scenery. He composed oratorios for a Catholic group called the Oratorian congregation in Rome. The organization was founded by the Italian priest and reformer Philip Neri (Filiippo Romolo de' Neri; 1515–1595).

Neri made friends easily, and in the late 1550s he began meeting regularly with some of them in his room, the "Oratory," at the church of San Girolamo della Carità. Neri dreaded formality and loved spontaneity. He gave his little groups a definite character with Scripture readings, short commentaries, brief prayers, and hymns. Palestrina set many of the scriptural texts to music, creating the "oratorio"—named for Neri's room, the Oratory—a form of musical presentation that is still popular today.

Did he "save" music?

Palestrina wrote his works during a period of change in the Roman Catholic Church. From 1545 to 1565, the church held a series of meetings called the Council of Trent. The purpose of the council was to initiate reforms at every level of religious life. A frequent topic of discussion was simplifying the music used in the liturgy, or church service. Some officials even suggested totally eliminating polyphonic music because it was too elaborate and secular, or nonreligious, and distracted from the solemnity of the worship service. In 1562 the council issued a canon, or church law stating that all secular matter must be removed from liturgical music. While music should be pleasing to the ear, it must also be simple and direct, having no embellishments that would interfere with an understanding of the text. Historians have speculated that Palestrina composed his masses to fit the reformers' requirements. An example is the *Missa Papae Marcelli*. According to one story, Palestrina "saved the art of music" with this work by dedicating it to Marcellus, who advocated reform. There seems to be no evidence that Palestrina deliberately modified his compositions, however, for scholars point out that he never showed any real interest in highly dramatic or experimental sacred music. It is known, though, that Palestrina's works were performed for, and approved by, Cardinal Carlo Borromeo (1538–1584). Borromeo was charged with making certain that liturgical music was free of secular tunes and unintelligible texts.

Palestrina was also consulted on musical matters by church officials. In a papal order of 1577, Palestrina and a colleague, Annibale Zoilo, were directed to revise the *Graduale*

Orlando di Lasso

An important Renaissance composer was Orlando di Lasso (c. 1530–1594). He was born in Mons, a city in present-day Belgium. Lasso spent most of his career in Italy and at the chapel of Holy Roman Emperor Charles V. A far more dramatic composer than his Italian contemporary Palestrina, Lasso wrote in every musical form and in a wide variety of styles.

Lasso was committed to the idea that music should heighten and convey the meaning of a text. Although he did not compose instrumental music, he excelled in all musical forms of his day—motets, masses, magnificats (music based on the song of Mary in the book of Luke from the Bible), madrigals, and songs. The most famous and admired composer in Europe in the late sixteenth century, Lasso was hailed early in his career as "prince of music" and "le divin Orlande" (divine Orlando). He was known for his talent for expressing the meaning of words in music. In fact, his music can be understood only in the context of the words that it so vividly presents. He accomplished this by a variety of means, sometimes through sudden changes in rhythm, melody, or harmony. Lasso rarely experimented with the latest musical trends, so by the end of his life, his style was overtaken by newer techniques. Nevertheless, he was the first great composer whose fame was spread by printed music. During his lifetime and soon after his death, more than six hundred publications featured his music. That is, between 1555 and 1595 a composition by Lasso appeared in print on the average of once a month in France, Italy, the Low Countries, or the German empire.

Romanum, the list of liturgical music used by the church. Their job was to purge all of the secular tunes that had accumulated over the centuries. Palestrina never did complete this laborious task. A new list, the Medicean Gradual, was released in the early seventeenth century. Although it is sometimes thought to be Palestrina's work, it was actually compiled by others. Since the Renaissance, Palestrina has been regarded as one of the foremost composers of sacred music. Yet his reputation suffered somewhat at the end of the nineteenth century, when his works were reduced to a set of composition "rules" by music teachers at academies and universities. Subsequent generations of young composers thus produced "Palestrinian" music that failed to meet the standards of free expression that the master achieved in his own compositions.

For More Information

Books

King, Ethel M. *Palestrina: the Prince of Music*. Brooklyn, N.Y.: Theo. Gaus' Sons, 1965.

Web Sites

Boynick, Matt. "Palestrina, G. P." *Classical Music Pages*. [Online] Available http://w3.rz-berlin.mpg.de/cmp/palestrina.html, April 5, 2002.

"Palestrina, G. P." *HyperMusic*. [Online] Available http://www.crosswinds.net/~musichistory/comp/palestrina.html, April 5, 2002.

Andrea Palladio

1508
Padua, Italy
1580
Venice, Italy

Architect

Andrea Palladio is one of the architects most closely associated with the Renaissance. The Renaissance was a cultural revolution that began in Italy in the mid-1300s. It was initiated by scholars called humanists who promoted the human-centered values of ancient Greece and Rome. Humanist ideals were soon influencing the arts, literature, philosophy, science, religion, and politics in Italy. His main contribution to architecture was the villa, or large country house, which became popular throughout Europe. Palladio was also involved in promoting the classical style developed by Italian architects in the fifteenth century. They refurbished old buildings and constructed new ones according to architectural details found in Roman ruins. Features of this style included simple but impressive building shapes, columns from the three basic classical orders (Corinthian, Doric, and Ionic), porticos (entrance porches), and loggias (roofed open galleries overlooking courtyards). Palladio adapted many of these features in his villas.

Begins career as architect

Palladio was born Andrea di Pietro della Gondola in Padua, Italy, in 1508. At age thirteen he was apprenticed to (hired to learn a trade) a local stonemason, a craftsman who makes or builds objects from stone. By 1524 Palladio had moved to Vincenza and formally registered in the guild (an association of craftsmen, merchants, and professionals that trained apprentices and set standards of production or business operation) of stonemasons. Palladio joined a workshop run by Giovanni di Giacomo da Porlezza and Girolamo Pittoni da Lumignano. Porlezza specialized in architecture, and Palladio continued working with him after leaving the workshop. By 1537 Palladio had entered the circle of Gian Giorgio Trissino (1478–1550), an aristocrat who had retired to Vincenza. Trissino gathered an academy of intellectually promising young men from the area into his villa.

Trissino had an important impact on Palladio. Through Trissino he was first exposed to humanist education (the study of literary masterpieces of ancient Greece and Rome) and learned Latin. He was also introduced to the treatise on architecture by Marcellus Vitruvius Pollio (called Vitruvius; first century B.C.), the ancient Roman architect and engineer. Through Trissino he became acquainted with many important intellectuals. The name Palladio, which he adopted in about 1545, came from Trissino's circle. In the 1540s Palladio visited Rome at least five times, often in the company of Trissino. During a trip taken between 1546 and 1547 he met the great sculptor and painter **Michelangelo** (1475–1564; see entry). Preserved drawings show that Palladio spent much of his time in Rome studying and surveying the Roman ruins.

Palladio's study of Roman ruins led him to pursue a career as an architect in the late 1530s. The breakthrough in his career came toward the end of the 1540s, when the city council of Vicenza commissioned him to complete the facade, or front, of the Basilica—the city's public palace. The Basilica is actually a complex of medieval buildings that were reorganized into a single structure during the fifteenth century. It had been surrounded by arcades (arched passageways with roofs) in a medieval style called Gothic. The arcades collapsed soon after they were completed in 1496. During the next fifty years city leaders looked for an architect to design a new facade in the Renaissance style. In 1546 Palladio submitted as plan in which he resolved the structural problems by redesigning the facade in the simple style used by the ancient Romans and by Italian architects in the fifteenth century.

Develops distinctive villa style

It took three years for the city council to approve Palladio's plans for the Basilica. Since the building was so large, work proceeded slowly and the entire project was not completed until 1614, nearly twenty-five years after Palladio's death. However, this work provided important contacts for Palladio and gained him a considerable reputation. He designed palazzos, or palaces, in Vincenza and began developing the villa type that later became identified with his name. A series of villas built during the 1550s and 1560s represent the model that is associated with Palladio. All of these villas have a vaulted *sala,* or central hall, that can be square, rectangular, or in the shape of a cross or the letter "T." A row of rooms lines each side of the *sala,* and the facade has a Greco-Roman (a Roman style influenced by the Greeks) temple portico (a type of porch with a roof supported by columns). A few villas have an upper story, in which the same design is repeated.

The popularity of the villa resulted from changes in the Venetian economy and an increasing trend toward agriculture. Villas functioned as homes for noblemen on agricultural estates. Palladio's most famous structure was the Villa Rotonda, known also as Villa Capra, which was built in the late 1560s for the retired papal secretary Paolo Almerico. Located on a hill near Vicenza, the villa had a dome-covered central hall with four big rooms in the corners and four smaller rooms next to them. Four identical porticoes open on all four facades. Over the centuries, the Rotonda became the prime example of Palladio's architecture and has been copied many times in various parts of the world.

Publishes important book

Throughout his career Palladio maintained contacts with humanists. Among them was Daniele Barbaro (1513–1570), a scholar and member of the Venetian high nobility. The patron (financial supporter) of several artists, Barbaro

Filippo Brunelleschi: First Renaissance Architect

Filippo Brunelleschi (1377–1446) is considered the first Renaissance architect. His refined classical style was inspired by twelfth-century Tuscan architecture and by the buildings of ancient Rome. Brunelleschi is also credited with developing the concept of linear perspective, also called one-point perspective, which influenced the depiction of space in painting and sculpture until the late nineteenth century. Linear perspective is a system derived from mathematics in which all elements of a composition are measured and arranged from a single point of view, or perspective.

Brunelleschi was born in Florence and began his career as a goldsmith. In 1401 he entered the competition for designing a new set of doors for the Baptistery (building used for baptism) of Florence Cathedral, but the commission was awarded to Lorenzo Ghiberti (c. 1378–1455). In 1417 he and other master goldsmiths presented opinions on the design and construction of the great dome that was to be built atop Florence Cathedral. It was perhaps at this time that Brunelleschi devised the method

of linear perspective, which he illustrated in two panels that are now lost. One panel depicted the Baptistery as viewed from the cathedral entrance, and the other illustrated the Palazzo Vecchio (the Medicis' palace).

Beginning in 1418 Brunelleschi concentrated on architecture. The following year he designed the loggia (an open, roofed porchlike structure with arches that overlooks a courtyard) of the Ospedale degli Innocenti (a hospital for orphans), which is usually considered the first Renaissance building. In 1420 Brunelleschi began to erect the Florence Cathedral dome in collaboration with Ghiberti, who eventually withdrew from the project. After returning to Florence in 1434 Brunelleschi worked on central-plan churches. Considered the ideal design during the Renaissance, this type of church is in the shape of a Greek cross, with four equal wings extending from a central circle. Brunelleschi died at Florence in 1446 and received the unusual honor of being buried in Florence Cathedral. Brunelleschi's architecture remained influential in Florence through the sixteenth century.

helped Palladio establish his reputation and introduced him to prospective Venetian clients. Palladio also designed a villa for Barbaro and Barbaro's brother Marcantonio. By the mid-1550s Palladio was working on *Four Books on Architecture,* which he published in 1570. Book One of this work discusses elements of architecture and the theory of the classical orders. Book Two presents plans for residential buildings Palladio designed. Book Three describes a number of bridges Palladio designed and gives an account of his work on the Basilica in Vicenza. Book Four contains Palladio's surveys of Roman temples.

During the latter part of his career he began working on churches. His greatest ecclesiastical, or religious, building was the church of San Giorgio Maggiore, which was started in 1566. In 1570 Palladio succeeded Jacopo Sansovino (1486–1570) as the main architectural adviser for the Republic of Venice. The ten years from this appointment until his death in 1580 were marked by one grand project, the church of Redentore in Venice. Many scholars consider Palladio to be the foremost Renaissance architect. The influence of his *Four Books on Architecture* is second only to that of *Regola delli cinque ordini d'architttura* (Canon of the five orders of architecture; 1563) by the architectural theorist Giacomo Barozzi da Vignola (1507–1573). Vignola's work was a detailed description of classical architecture and served as a manual for the education of Renaissance architects. Palladio's book shifted the focus from theory to practice by showing how classical ideas were used in Renaissance buildings.

Palladio's designs were often copied, and his innovative use of classical architecture became common practice. Palladio had an immense influence on architects in Italy. By the seventeenth century his ideas had also arrived in England through the efforts of the English designer Inigo Jones (1573–1652). Soon Palladio's style was spreading across Europe, and it reached the American colonies in the eighteenth century. Interest in Palladio's work did not wane even in the twentieth century, when architects were again focusing on his use of classical details.

For More Information

Books

Ackerman, James S. *Palladio's Villas*. Locust Valley, N.Y.: Institute of Fine Arts, New York University, 1967.

Farber, Joseph C. *Palladio's Architecture and its Influence: A Photographic Guide*. New York: Dover Publications, 1980.

Web Sites

"Palladio, Andrea." *Encyclopedia.com*. [Online] Available http://encyclopedia.com/searchpool.asp?target=@DOCTITLE%20Palladio%20%20Andrea, April 5, 2002.

"Palladio, Andrea." *Palladian Buildings in Vicenza.* [Online] Available http://www.ashmm.com/cultura/palladio/copertuk.htm, April 5, 2002.

Palladio, Andrea—Palladio and Pattern Books. [Online] Available http://mondrian.princeton.edu/Campus/text_pattern.html, April 5, 2002.

Theophrastus Paracelsus

1493
Einsiedeln, Switzerland
1541
Salzburg, Austria

Physician and reformer

Theophrastus Paracelsus.
Reproduced by permission of
Archive Photos, Inc.

The Swiss-born physician Theophrastus Paracelsus is considered the first to use chemicals to treat disease. His ideas were not widely accepted until the seventeenth century, when physicians and chemists studied his works and incorporated his methods into mainstream European medicine.

Paracelus's actual name was Phillippus Aureolus Theophrastus Bombastus von Hohenheim. After his death he was commonly known as Theophrastus Paracelsus or simply Paracelsus. He was born in Einsiedeln, a village in Switzerland, where his German father practiced medicine. His mother, a native of the village, served at a nearby monastery. After his mother's death, Paracelsus and his father moved to Villach, in a mining region of Carinthia. Paracelsus claimed that he was tutored by his father and various priests, including Abbot Johannes Trithermius (also called Heidenberg; 1462–1516), who was well known as an occult philosopher (one who studies the action or influence of supernatural or supranormal powers or some secret knowledge of them).

Wanders throughout Europe

Paracelsus's written work shows his wide-ranging informal education, which included religious studies, medical knowledge, and an acquaintance with the ideas of late medieval mysticism (intense awareness of supernatural forces). He was also acquainted with Neoplatonism, a philosophical movement of the Renaissance that revived the ideas of the ancient Greek philosopher Plato (428–c. 347 B.C.). In addition, he studied alchemy, a medieval science devoted to turning base metals into gold, finding a universal cure for disease, and prolonging life. Paracelsus demonstrated knowledge of folk-healing methods, popular superstitions, and widespread beliefs about the sources of good and evil in the world. Although he knew some Latin and was able to converse on the basic theories of academic medicine, he had unconventional ideas regarding human anatomy (structure of the body), human reproduction (functions of male and female bodies in the production of offspring), and natural philosophy (natural sciences, such as physics, chemistry, and biology). On the basis of this knowledge about Paracelsus's work, historians suggest he did not attend a university long enough to earn a degree. Paracelsus was one of the many religious thinkers and reformers who wandered throughout Europe in the early sixteenth century. He extended his travels into Russia and the Middle East (countries in southwest Asia and North Africa). After practicing as a physician in Germany and Switzerland, he settled in Salzburg, Austria.

Paracelsus's writings show that he was immersed in the social and intellectual turmoil of the radical Reformation. This was a movement led by religious reformers who called for more drastic changes in the Roman Catholic Church than those advocated by **Martin Luther** (1483–1546; see entry), the German priest whose "Ninety-Five Theses" triggered the Protestant Reformation. Paracelsus's involvement is shown by his behavior at Salzburg, where he narrowly avoided prosecution for supporting the rebel cause in the violently suppressed Peasants' War. The Peasants' War was a series of revolts that began in Germany in 1524 and then spread across central Europe as Protestant peasants expressed discontent with their lack of social and political rights. Like other radical reformers, Paracelsus gave mystical interpretations to the Trinity, the three aspects of the Christian God: the Father, the Son, and the Holy Spirit.

Challenges medical authorities

Although Paracelsus's religious beliefs are evident in his writings, he had a more direct influence on the ideas of the next two generations of physicians. He is remembered primarily for questioning the medical theories of the ancient Greek thinkers Aristotle (384–322 B.C.) and Galen (A.D. 129–c. 199). Their ideas had been interpreted by the Islamic philosopher and scientist Avicenna (Ibn Sīnā; 980–1037), who wrote more than two hundred scientific works that greatly influenced medicine. Avicenna's concepts were fiercely upheld by elite professors in colleges of medicine throughout Europe. In 1527, during a student midsummer celebration at the university in Basel, Switzerland, Paracelsus threw Avicenna's *Canon of Medicine* onto a bonfire. It was one of the most expensive textbooks used at the university. That year Paracelsus had been hired as the Basel municipal physician, a post that permitted him to give public lectures. His use of that privilege to challenge accepted ideas made him unpopular in the medical establishment.

In particular, Paracelsus strongly disagreed with the theory of humors introduced by the ancient Greek physician Hippocrates (460–370 B.C.) and the theory of temperaments later developed by Galen (see accompanying box). Paracelsus thought the treatments based on these theories were ineffective against new diseases that were ravaging Europe. Paracelsus believed that diseases were specific ailments and could be cured with specific remedies. He advocated the use of powerful drugs that in many cases were made through the distillation of toxic, or poisonous, material and plants. Perfected in the Middle Ages (c. 400–1400), distillation is the process of producing a solvent by purifying a liquid through evaporation and condensation at high temperatures in a furnace. Paracelsus was among the first to utilize a new furnace design that improved the process and produced better solvents for medical purposes. For this reason he is regarded today as a pioneer of healing chemistry, called iatrochemistry. He also emphasized the value of observation and experience in the treatment of disease. He is credited with recognizing the medicinal benefits of opium, mercury, lead, sulfur, iron, arsenic, and copper sulfate. The theory of healing chemistry, as well as Paracelsus's methods of using it, was not well received during his lifetime, and even considered dangerous by some

Humors

The theory of humors was introduced by the ancient Greek physician Hippocrates, who is considered the "father" of medicine. According to Hippocrates, the body is composed of four fluids, or humors—blood, phlegm, black bile, and yellow bile. He believed these humors control a human being's health, and an imbalance causes illness, disease, and pain. Good health, he argued, is achieved through a perfect balance of the humors. Since most illnesses are caused by an excess of a particular humor, good health could be achieved by reducing the amount found in the body. To produce such a balance, a physician usually examined a patient's astrological chart, not his or her body. (An astrological chart is a prediction of future events made by an astrologer on the basis of observations of the positions of the stars and planets.) After reading the chart the physician would give the patient a blood-letting (draining of blood from the body), most commonly through the use of leeches (blood-sucking worms). Hippocrates's theory of humors was the standard medical practice for centuries.

The Greek physician Galen introduced a new aspect of this theory when he suggested that there were four basic temperaments, or behaviors, determined by the humors: the sanguine, or healthy, type corresponds to the blood; the phlegmatic, or sluggish, type is related to phlegm; the choleric, or hot-tempered, type is associated with black bile; and the melancholic, or depressed, type correlates with yellow bile. A person's psychology, or mental state, as well as health was explained in terms of the humors until the nineteenth century, when Rudolf Virchow (1821–1902) presented his ideas on cellular pathology (diseases transmitted in the cells of the body). As a result of Virchow's ideas, the theory of humors was then abandoned.

critics. Alarmed medical authorities took steps to discredit Paracelsus in public. In 1528, while suing a rich citizen in an attempt to collect an exorbitant medical bill, Paracelsus fled Basel and resumed his life of wandering. After practicing medicine in various places in Germany and Switzerland, he finally settled in Salzburg, where he produced his written works. He died in Salzburg in 1541.

Considered a thinker ahead of his time

Paracelsus's scholarly reputation was damaged by his unsettled life, lack of education, and acceptance of questionable medical practices and heretical religious ideas. Few of his treatises were published in his lifetime. Although he wrote in German—as opposed to Latin, which was the traditional language for scholarly works—his ideas were difficult to understand. If it were not for the next generation of medical scholars and publishers, who worked hard to interpret what Paracelsus was talking about, his theories would have had little impact on the scientific and medical world of the seventeenth century.

Among those who accepted Paraclesian medicine was Gerard Dorn (died 1584). He located, edited, and published Paracelsus's medical and philosophical manuscripts, sometimes even writing works under the master's name. Dorn interpreted Paracelsus's theories in the light of Neoplatonic philosophy, which reached its height in the sixteenth century. Dorn defended Paracelsus against the vigorous attacks of the Swiss theologian and physician Thomas Erastus (Thomas Lüber; 1524–1583), who condemned Paracelsus's theories as not only heretical but also an attack on university-supported medicine. Dorn compiled a dictionary of Paraclesus's peculiar terminology, which was reprinted and translated into several languages.

The Champions of Paracelsus

Petrus Severinus (c. 1542–1602), Dorn's younger contemporary, wrote *Ideal of Philosophical Medicine* (1571), in which he interpreted Paracelsus's theories so they could be used along with those of Hippocrates, Galen, and Aristotle. Severinus wanted to create a frame of well-articulated biological theory that explained the physiology and pathology (disease) of the organic world in terms of spiritual forces and divinely ordained patterns of development. His book inspired Oswald Croll (1560–1609) and Johann Hartmann (1568–1631) to make Paracelsian medical concepts and drugs the foundation of seventeenth-century medicine. Croll wrote *Basilica chymica* (1609), a popular introduction to chemical methods and recipes for preparing Paraclesian-style medicaments (substances used in therapy). Severinus's vision of Paraclesian "vital philosophy" was adopted by Hartman, who is regarded as the holder of the first university chair in chemistry (at Marburg, Germany, in 1609). Hartmann taught medical chemistry as a laboratory subject and later expanded Croll's book.

As a result of the work of these scholars and chemists, chemical drugs were accepted by European pharmacists and even adopted by Galenic physicians. Chemical physicians, who were trained in laboratory methods and followed new principles of medical treatment, provided an alternative to the classical methods of medicine that were taught in the universities. By the end of the seventeenth century, chemical treatments described in Paracelsus's works were absorbed into mainstream medicine. Paracelsus is now considered the first to connect goiter (swelling of the thyroid gland) with minerals in drinking water and the first to describe syphilis (a contagious sexually transmitted disease). Paracelus introduced the therapeutic use of mineral baths. He was also the first to describe silicosis (disease of the lungs caused by inhaling dusts), and his work *On Diseases of Miners* was the first study devoted to an occupational disease (disease caused by a work environment). In 1752 the city of Salzburg erected a statue in Paracelsus's honor.

For More Information

Books

Webster, Charles. *From Paracelsus to Newton: Magic and the Making of Modern Science.* New York: Cambridge University Press, 1982.

Web Sites

Debus, Allen G. *Paracelsus, Theophrastus—Medical Revolution.* [Online] Available http://www.nlm.nih.gov/exhibition/paracelsus/paracelsus _2.html, April 5, 2002.

"Paracelsus, Theophrastus." *Coelum Philosophorum.* [Online] Available http://www.levity.com/alchemy/coelum.html, January 3, 2002.

Francesco Petrarch

July 20, 1304
Arezzo, Italy
July 1374
Padua, Italy

Poet

"Rome was greater than I thought, and so are its remains. Now I wonder not that the world was ruled by this city but that the rule came so late."

Petrarch.

The Italian poet Petrarch is considered the founder of humanism, a movement devoted to the revival of ancient Greek and Roman literature and philosophy. He has been called the first modern man because he wrote about the external world and analyzed his own thoughts and emotions. Conscious of the fleeting nature of human existence, Petrarch felt his mission was to save works by classical authors for future generations. He also popularized the sonnet form and is considered by many to be the first modern poet. Petrarch's personal letters mark a distinct break with medieval traditions and a return to the classical and early Christian practice of private letter writing. He provided the great stimulus to the cultural movement that culminated in the Renaissance in the fifteenth and sixteenth centuries.

Writes early poems

Petrarch was born Francesco Petrarca in Arezzo, Italy, to Pietro di Parenzo and Eletta Canigiani. His father, usually called Ser Petracco, was a notary (public clerk). In 1302, the year Petrarch was born, Ser Petracco was falsely accused of corruption in public office and he went to his hometown of Incisa. Early in 1305 Eletta and Petrarch joined Petracco in Incisa, where they remained for six years. Petrarch's brother Gherardo was born there in 1307. In 1311 the family moved to Pisa, and the following year they settled in Carpentras, France, near Avignon. At that time Avignon was the home of the pope, the supreme head of the Roman Catholic Church, and the seat of the Holy Roman Empire. In 1307 the papacy (office of the pope) and the imperial headquarters had been relocated from Rome, Italy, to Avignon after conflict within the church. Beginning in 1316 Petrarch pursued legal studies at the University of Montpellier, but he preferred reading classical poetry to studying law. During this time his mother died. To mark the sorrowful occasion, Petrarch composed a poem in Latin, the earliest of his works to have survived. In 1320, along with Gherardo, he went to the University of Bologna, the oldest university in Europe. Although Petrarch excelled in his studies, he realized that he did not want to be a lawyer. After his father died in 1326 he abandoned law and participated in the fashionable social life of Avignon.

Petrarch Perfects Sonnet

Petrarch perfected the verse form called the sonnet in his *Canzoniere*. During the Renaissance poets throughout Europe adapted the Petrarchan sonnet to their own forms.

The sonnet was not original to Petrarch. It was invented by Giacomo da Lentino, a notary at the court of Holy Roman Emperor Frederick II in the first half of the thirteenth century. It was probably derived from the eight-line Sicilian peasant song, the *canzuna,* or the eight-line literary verse called the *strambotto.* To the eight-line form Giacoma added six lines to create what is now known as the sonnet. He wrote a total of fifteen sonnets. The form was imitated through a poetic debate involving a sonnet by Jacopo Mostacci, a sonnet by Pier della Vigna, and two sonnets by the abbot (head of an abbey) of Tivoli. These nineteen poems are considered the beginning of the tradition of writing sonnets.

On April 6, 1327, in the church of Saint Clare, Petrarch saw and fell in love with a young woman whom he called Laura. She did not return his love. The true identity of Laura is not known, but there is no doubt regarding her existence or the intensity of the poet's passion. He began writing the *Canzoniere* (Song book), a series of love lyrics inspired by Laura. In these poems he departed from the medieval convention of seeing a woman as a spiritual symbol and depicted Laura as a real person. Petrarch is credited with perfecting the sonnet in the *Canzoniere* (see accompanying box).

Begins service in the church

In 1330 Petrarch and Gherardo found themselves rapidly running through their inheritance. Having rejected law and then medicine as professions, Petrarch had to find other employment. Upon the recommendation of an influential friend, both Petrarch and his brother entered the service of Cardinal Giovanni Colonna. In 1333, motivated by intellectual curiosity, Petrarch traveled to France, Flanders (a country in present-day Belgium, France, and the Netherlands), and Germany. Upon returning to Avignon, he met the scholar Dionigi di Borgo San Sepolcro, who made him aware of early Christian literature. Until the end of his life, Petrarch carried with him a tiny copy of the *Confessions* of Saint Augustine (an early church father), a gift from Dionigi. In 1336 Petrarch climbed Mount Ventoux in Provence, France. When he arrived at the top of the mountain, he opened the *Confessions* at random, reading that men admire mountains and rivers and seas and stars, only to neglect themselves. He described this experience in spiritual terms in a letter that he wrote to Dionigi.

In 1335, on the recommendation of Colonna, Pope Benedict XII (died 1342; reigned 1334–42) named Petrarch a canon (administrative official) at the cathedral of Lombex. This appointment provided him an income without requiring him to remain at the cathedral itself. Over the next few years Petrarch traveled widely and continued writing poetry. In late 1336 he visited Rome for the first time. The ancient ruins of the city deepened his admiration for the classical age. What is important to note is that some time before his appointment, Petrarch had written a long letter in Latin verse to Benedict XII, in which he strongly encouraged the pope to return to Rome. This is the first indication of Petrarch's firm belief that Rome was the rightful seat of the papacy and the Holy Roman Empire. (In 1307, following a power struggle among cardinals, the papacy, or office of the pope, was moved to Avignon, France.) His visit only served to strengthen this belief.

In 1337 Petrarch returned to France and went to live at Vaucluse, where he led a solitary life and composed his

Coluccio Salutati

After Petrarch, Coluccio Salutati (1331–1406) was the most important Italian humanist. He introduced the concept of civic humanism, which emphasized a humanist education for government officials and supported republican values (representative rule). Salutati began his career around 1350 as a private notary in the area around his hometown of Stignano. By 1358 he was the leading political figure in his local commune (district governed by a group of leaders called a corporation). Early in 1374 Salutati was summoned to Florence to take up the newly created position of secretary of the Tratte, which supervised the republic's elaborate procedures for electing government officials by lot, or random chance. He was probably involved with the group that removed the chancellor (head official), Niccolò Monachi, from office the following year. Salutati then combined the position of chancellor with the Tratte and became the new leader of the Republic of Florence. At that time Florence was at war with the papacy over control of the republic. Salutati became internationally famous through the brilliance of his *missive,* or public letters, which he wrote to defend Florence's cause. Over the next thirty-one years he may have produced

tens of thousands of letters, of which about five thousand remain.

Although Salutati showed an interest in ancient literature and history, his approach to the ancients was different from that of Petrarch. Petrarch felt nostalgia for the ancient world, whereas Salutati was comfortable in the fourteenth century and did not accept Petrarch's notion of the "dark ages." For Salutati the centuries between antiquity and the present had witnessed only a gradual decay in learning. Petrarch preferred to study and translate Greek and Roman texts in scholarly seclusion, but Salutati promoted humanist ideals in public life. He argued that a political leader should have a knowledge of history and obtain a humanist education. Largely through Salutati's efforts, Florence became the capital of the humanist movement in the first half of the fifteenth century. Particularly important was Salutati's role in reintroducing Greek learning to western Europe. In 1397 he was instrumental in bringing the Greek scholar Manuel Chrysoloras to Florence. When Chrysoloras went on to Padua three years later, he left behind students who could work in the Greek language on their own.

major Latin works. Four years later he was crowned poet laureate in Rome. He delivered a famous oration (an elaborate discourse delivered in a formal and dignified manner) that demonstrated his ability to combine aspects of classical poetry with his own verse. The fame Petrarch had achieved in this single event was immeasurable. He was a celebrity wherever he went and was in demand as the honored guest in cities throughout Europe. He became the best-known private citizen in Europe. In 1337 Petrarch also wrote a letter to Colonna recalling the ancient sites they had seen together in Rome. In the letter he stated that the reign of Roman Emperor Constantine (died 337; ruled 306–37), rather than the birth of Jesus of Nazareth (also called the Christ; the founder of Christianity), was the great dividing point in history. Constantine was the last ruler of the Roman Empire, and Petrarch considered the fall of the Roman Empire to be the end of Western (non-Asian) culture. Petrarch gave the name "dark age" to the period that followed the end of Constantine's reign in the fourth century and continued until Petrarch's own time. Petrarch used the term "dark age" because he believed nothing of cultural significance happened during those centuries. Petrarch thus originated the concept of three major periods in Western (non-Asian) history: ancient, medieval, modern. (The Middle Ages, or medieval period, is often called the "Dark Ages.")

Calls Avignon the Babylonian captivity

The year 1343 was a momentous one for Petrarch. He met Cola di Rienzo (1313–1354), who would later serve at the papal court in Avignon. In January 1343 Petrarch's royal sponsor died. His brother Gherardo also joined the Carthusians (a religious order founded by Saint Bruno), causing Petrarch to examine his own life and goals. In 1343 Petrarch's illegitimate (child born to parents who are not legally married) daughter, Francesca, was born. Out of these troubles arose his soul-searching imaginary dialogue with Saint Augustine, *Secretum,* as well as his seven penitential (the showing of penitence, or remorse) psalms and his treatise on the cardinal, or chief, virtues, *Rerum memorandarum libri* (Books of Memorable Things).

Over the next few years Petrarch traveled throughout Italy. In 1345, at the cathedral library in Verona, he discovered letters of the ancient Roman statesman Marcus Tullius Cicero (106–43 B.C.). Petrarch personally copied these letters. By 1348 Petrarch was in Parma, where he received news of Laura's death. That year the Black Death (a widespread outbreak of disease) deprived Petrarch of several of his close friends, among them Colonna. Petrarch wrote several letters reflecting on the ravages of the plague. His discovery of Cicero's letters had inspired him to begin a collection of his own Latin prose letters in 1350. The result was twenty-four books titled *Epistolae familiares* (Letters on familiar matters), seventeen books titled *Seniles* (Letters of riper years), seventeen letters titled *Sine nomine* (Book without a name), and three books titled *Epistolae metricae* (Metrical letters).

Since 1350 was a Year of Jubilee (special spiritual celebration held every twenty-five years by the Catholic Church), Petrarch also made a pilgrimage, or religious journey, to Rome. On his way he stopped in Florence, where he made new friends. Among them was Giovanni Boccaccio (1313–1375), who wrote *Decameron,* a work that influenced Renaissance literature. In 1351 Petrarch returned to Avignon, but two years later he left France and settled in Milan. He had become increasingly troubled by the presence of the papacy in Avignon. Petrarch argued that the Catholic Church was being held hostage in France, much as the ancient Jews were held captive in Babylon, and he called the Avignon papacy the "Babylonian captivity." Petrarch was referring to the Babylonian captivity of the Jewish people as described in the Old Testament of the Bible (the Christian holy book) in the Book of Jeremiah, Chapter 20, verse 4. In 586 B.C. the city of Jerusalem, which was the capital of the Jewish empire, fell to the Babylonians. An unknown number of Jews—some estimates place the total in the thousands—were deported, or forcibly sent, to Babylonia.

Final years are productive

Petrarch remained in Milan for eight years, where he was supported by the Visconti family, particularly by Archbishop Galeazzo II Visconti (1321–1378). Although many friends criticized Petrarch for living under an autocracy (a system of rule in which one person has unlimited power), he was pleased with his position, which allowed him to do whatever he liked. One of the projects he began in Milan turned into his longest work, *De remediis utriusque fortune* (Remedies for good and bad fortune). In the book he discussed good and bad fortune by personifying (giving human, or personal, attributes to emotions) Joy, Hope, Reason, Sorrow, Fear, and Adversity. During his stay in Milan, Petrarch had extensive dealings with

Holy Roman Emperor Charles IV (1316–1378; ruled 1355–78). Petrarch renewed his pleas for the government to return to Rome and reestablish the city as the seat of the Empire. The eight years that Petrarch spent in Milan represent the longest period he remained in one place. He completed *De remediis* and made progress in compiling the *Canzoniere* and *Familiares*.

Although Petrarch promoted writing in the Italian language, he regarded *Canzoniere* and his other Italian poems as less important than his Latin works. He had mastered Latin as a living language, producing the great epic (long poem) *Africa*, which described the virtues of the Roman Republic. Among his other important Latin works were *Metrical Epistles, On Contempt for the Worldly Life, On Solitude, Ecologues,* and *Letters*. Petrarch's sense of himself as an individual and his desire for personal earthly immortality had an impact on other humanists, who realized they were living at the end of a long dark age. The influence of Petrarch's art and reflective approach was felt for more than three centuries in all European literature.

In 1361 Petrarch went to Padua because the plague, which took the lives of his son and several friends, had broken out in Milan. In Padua he terminated the *Familiares* and initiated a new collection, *Seniles*. The following year he settled in Venice, where he had been given a house in exchange for the bequest (gift in a will) of his library to the city. In 1368 he was given some land in the community of Arquà near Padua, and a house was finished in 1370. Failing health limited his travels, although he was able to take periodic trips, mainly carrying out diplomatic missions for the ruler of Padua, Francesco da Carrara (died 1393). Petrarch spent his final years completing collections of his poems and letters. He died in 1374 and was buried in a marble tomb in the parish church at Arquà.

For More Information

Books

Petrarca, Francesco. *Selections from "Canzoniere" and Other Works*. Mark Musa, editor. New York: Oxford University Press, 1999.

Web Sites

"Petrarch, Francesco." *Encyclopedia.com.* [Online] Available http://www.encyclopedia.com/searchpool.asp?target=@DOCTITLE%20Petrarch, April 5, 2002.

"Petrarch, Francesco: Letters, circa 1372." *Medieval Sourcebook*. [Online] Available http://www.fordham.edu/halsall/source/petrarch1.html, April 5, 2002.

Petrarch's House. [Online] Available http://freia.dei.unipd.it/civici/civici/petra%24.html, April 5, 2002.

Philip II

May 21, 1527
Valladolid, Spain
September 13, 1598
El Escorial, Spain

King

Philip II was king of Spain from 1556 to 1598. During his reign the Spanish empire was severely challenged, and its economic, social, and political institutions strained almost to the breaking point.

Inherits vast empire

Philip was born in Valladolid, Spain, on May 21, 1527. He was the son of Holy Roman Emperor **Charles V** (1500–1558; see entry). In 1543, at age sixteen, Philip married his cousin, Maria of Portugal. She lived only two years, leaving a son, Don Carlos. Charles then arranged for Philip to marry Mary I (called Bloody Mary; 1516–1558; ruled 1553–58) of England, the Catholic queen of a basically Protestant country. Charles did this to consolidate his empire. Philip moved to England, but his stay was not a happy one. Mary died in 1558 and was succeeded by her half-sister, **Elizabeth I** (1533–1603; see entry), who was committed to keeping England a Protestant nation. Charles V also died in 1558, and Philip inherited the larger portion of his father's dominions: Spain, the Low Countries (basically present-day Belgium and the Netherlands), Franche–Comté, Sicily and southern Italy, the duchy of Milan, and Spain's colonies in the New World (the European term for the Americas), including Mexico and much of South America. The rest of Charles's dominions was the Holy Roman Empire (Austria and parts of Germany), which he left to his brother Ferdinand (1503–1564; ruled 1558–64), who succeeded him as emperor.

Philip returned to Spain in 1559. In that year Spain and France signed the Cateau-Cambrésis peace treaty, which ended the Italian Wars (1494–1559), a conflict between the two countries over control of Italy. The war ended mainly because both Spain and France had run out of money, not as the result of a resolution of differences. The temporary harmony between the two powers was symbolized by Philip's marriage to Elizabeth of Valois (1545–1568), the daughter of the French king Henry II (1519–1559; ruled 1547–59) and his wife **Catherine de Médicis** (1519–1589; see entry). Elizabeth proved to be Philip's favorite wife. Philip was married four times: In 1543 to Maria of Portugal (died 1545), mother of Don Carlos; in 1554 to Mary I of England (1516–1558); in 1560 to Elizabeth of Valois, mother of the infants Isabella and Catalina; and in 1570 to Anna of Austria (died 1580), mother of the next king, Philip III.

Unlike Charles V, Philip did not travel extensively. Instead, he preferred to rule the country from his palaces. Philip was fair, soft-spoken, and had an icy self-mastery. In the words of one of his ministers, he had a smile that cut like a sword. He immersed himself in an ocean of paperwork, studying dispatches and documents and adding marginal comments on them while scores of other documents and dispatches piled up on tables. With the problems of communication in Philip's far-reaching empire, once a decision was made it could not be undone. As king, he preferred to reserve all final decisions for himself. He mistrusted powerful and independent personalities and rarely placed much confidence in aides. Philip devoted his private life to collecting art, cultivating flowers, and reading religious works. His main interest, however, was designing and building El Escorial, the royal palace outside Madrid. He was overjoyed when the huge complex was finally completed. A combination palace, monastery (religious house for men), and mausoleum (building that holds tombs), Escorial was Philip's preferred place for working.

Confronted with numerous problems

During the first twenty years of his reign, Philip was confronted with many problems. Charles had left him in charge of an unresolved war with the Muslim Turks, which had begun in 1551 over control of the Mediterranean Sea. The Muslim Turks were followers of the Islamic religion who lived in the Ottoman Empire, a vast kingdom in Asia and North Africa. For many centuries, the Muslims were viewed as an archenemy to the Europeans, who saw them as a threat to Christian dominance of Europe. In 1560 the Spanish attempted unsuccessfully to take Tripoli, a port city in northwest Lebanon, from the Turks. In 1563 and 1565, Philip's troops managed to repulse Turkish attacks on Oran, a port city in Algeria, and the island of Malta, a Spanish stronghold in the Mediterranean near Sicily. The conflict ended in 1571, when Philip's illegitimate (born out of wedlock) half-brother, John of Austria (1545–1578), led a Catholic armada (fleet of armored ships) against the Turks in the great naval battle of Lepanto (Gulf of Corinth) in the Ionian Sea off the coast of Greece. The Spaniards took 127 Ottoman ships and thousands of soldiers and seamen. As a result of John's victory, the Ottoman Empire was no longer a threat to Spain's rich possessions in Italy and along the Mediterranean.

While Spanish forces were defeating the Ottomans, Philip was contending with the Revolt of the Netherlands, which broke out in 1566. Though the revolt did not end with Dutch independence until 1648, the Spanish had many military victories in the Netherlands during Philip's reign. The uprising began when Dutch Protestants staged violent riots and smashed statues of Catholic saints. In 1567 Philip introduced the Spanish Inquisition (a court that sought out and punished heretics, or those who violated church laws) in the Netherlands. He then sent Fernando Álvarez de Toledo, duke of Alba (c. 1507–1582) to crush the revolt. Alba initiated an extremely repressive regime. Arresting two rebel leaders, Lamoral, count of Egmont (1522–1568), and Philip de Montmorency, count of Hoorn (c. 1518–1568), Alba established the Council of Troubles. Alba had Egmont and Hoorn executed along with perhaps twelve thousand other rebels. Other notable leaders fled to safety in Germany. Among them was William I Prince of Orange (1533–1584), the spiritual leader of the rebellion. Nevertheless, Alba's repression continued unchecked, until by

1573 Philip had seen enough. He recalled Alba and replaced him with Luis de Requesens (1528–1576). In 1577 Requesens was replaced by John of Austria (1547–1578).

In 1568, at the height of his Dutch troubles, Philip experienced several other misfortunes. He lost his third and most beloved wife, Elizabeth of Valois, as she was delivering a baby daughter. Philip's son, Carlos, was exhibiting bouts of severe mental instability. For instance, Carlos threw a servant out of a window when the young man crossed him. He frequently attacked his father's ministers, including the duke of Alba, with a knife. Carlos also made a shoemaker eat a pair of boots because they fit too tight. The troubled young man was finally locked away in a tower, where he went on a series of hunger strikes and died later in the year.

Defends Catholic faith

The Dutch troubles worsened in 1578 when Philip approved the assassination of Juan de Escobedo (died 1578), John of Austria's dangerous and ambitious secretary. Two years later, Philip issued a royal proclamation condemning William of Orange as an outlaw and the main source of unrest in the Netherlands. The king's announcement also offered a reward of 25,000 ducats (an amount of Spanish money) for the capture of William of Orange. Orange responded with a document that accused Philip of incest (having sexual relations with family members), adultery (having sexual relations outside marriage), and the murders of both Carlos and Elizabeth of Valois.

Philip was convinced, however, that God had chosen him for a special mission to defend the Catholic faith. Indeed, it seemed to many Europeans that "God had turned into a Spaniard" by 1584. That year an assassin killed William of Orange in his home in the Delft region. In 1585, Alessandro Farnese (1545–1592), the duke of Parma, surpassed the military skill of Alba when he captured the great walled town of Antwerp (a city in present-day Belgium). The successful siege ended a five-year Spanish offensive that conquered more than thirty rebel Dutch towns and maintained Spanish and Catholic control of the southern provinces of the Netherlands until 1714.

Meanwhile, in 1580, Philip had claimed the throne of Portugal. Forced to fight for what he considered to be his hereditary rights (his mother was the princess of Portugal), he had sent Alba into Portugal with twenty-two thousand troops. The old and brutal duke was again successful, and the vast dominions of Portugal fell into Philip's hands. Then in a crowning victory, Philip's navy, under Álvaro de Bázan (1526–1588), the marquis de Santa Cruz, smashed a combined English-French force off the coast of the Azores in 1582 and 1583. In the New World, Spanish conquistadors (conquerors) accomplished the "taming of America" by violently subduing various rival Native American groups. To many Europeans at the time, this was Philip's most impressive achievement.

Organizes "Invincible Armada"

Just as Philip was on the verge of reclaiming the northern provinces of the Netherlands, his attention was diverted by war with England. The English Protestant queen, Elizabeth I, was worried about the Catholic advance in the Low Countries. In 1585 she openly supported the Dutch rebels. Philip immediately began organizing the famous "Invincible Armada," a fleet of 130 heavily armored ships that carried 30,000 men, for an invasion of England. Leading the venture would be the experienced admiral, the marquis de Santa Cruz. The plan called for the Armada to sail from Lisbon, Portugal, into the English Channel. The ships would stop off the coast of Flanders and pick up the 22,000-man army led by the duke of Parma. The Armada would then sail on to England and stage a massive sea assault.

Almost from the beginning, things went wrong with the complicated Spanish plan. In 1587, even before the Armada could set out, the English seaman Francis Drake (c. 1540–1596) launched a surprise attack on the Spanish ships, which were anchored in the port of Cádiz, Spain. The destruction to the Armada was so great that the invasion was delayed for a year. In the meantime, Santa Cruz died and Philip replaced him with the inexperienced Alonso Pérez de Guzmán (c. 1550–1619), duke of Medina-Sidonia. Medina-Sidonia was an army commander, so he protested that he was unqualified to lead a naval fleet. Philip brushed

An illustration of Philip's "Invincible Armada."
©Bettmann/Corbis.
Reproduced by permission of Corbis Corporation.

his reservations aside, insisting that only a man of Medina-Sidonia's stature would be obeyed by the captains of the Armada ships.

England defeats Armada

In May 1588 the Spanish Armada set out from Lisbon, but storms forced the fleet into La Coruña in northwestern Spain. The ships did not set sail again until July. By this time Elizabeth had prepared the English fleet and organized a small but dedicated land army. In August, sailing against strong winds, the Armada began moving up the Channel toward Flanders. Medina-Sidonia had been ordered not to engage in battle with the English until he had made contact with Parma. This gave the advantage to the English main fleet, which departed from Plymouth and was sailing with the wind. Once within range of the Armada, the English ships were able to fire their weapons at the Spanish vessels from a relatively safe distance. The light and quick English ships also had the advantage of being able to outmaneuver the bulky Spanish galleons (ships powered by oars). The English made three assaults on the Spanish, but they did not inflict any serious damage. On August 6, Medina-Sidonia anchored his fleet at Calais to await contact with Parma. But Medina-Sidonia made a fatal mistake on the night of August 7. He had not secured all of the anchors, so some ships drifted in the water and left an opening for a squadron of English fire ships to move in and set the Armada ablaze. One by one the Spanish ships broke their cables and headed for open water. The smaller English ships darted in and out of the flames, pouncing on stragglers.

Then a powerful storm—the "Great Protestant Wind," as the English called it—swept through the Channel and forced the Spanish vessels away from England. Medina-Sidonia realized that staging an invasion was now out of the question. He did his best to save the fleet, and the Armada sailed north. Storm after storm seemed to come from nowhere to pound the galleons as they desperately tried to sail around the British Isles. Many of the Spanish ships broke up on the west coast of Ireland. Nearly three months after the battle, Geoffrey Felton, secretary for Ireland, went walking on the coast of Sligo Bay. Although the secretary had seen slaughter and bloodshed during Irish wars with the English, he reported that these horrors paled in comparison to the terrible sight of the bloated corpses of more than eleven hundred Spaniards that had been washed up onto the coast. Half of the armada was lost and so was Philip's dream of making England into a Catholic province.

In 1584 Philip began Spanish financial aid to France's Catholic League (an alliance formed by Catholics against Protestants in France), in an unsuccessful effort to put a Catholic on the throne of France. Philip II died in 1598, four months after making peace with France in the Treaty of Vervins. He believed he had left his son, King Philip III (1578–1621; ruled 1598–1621), relatively free from international difficulties. Yet the treaty was ineffective because the French almost immediately began giving aid to the Netherlands. Claiming also that the treaty applied only to the continent of Europe, the French continued to encroach on Spanish commerce in the Atlantic Ocean.

For More Information

Books
Kamen, Henry. *Philip of Spain*. New Haven, Conn.: Yale University Press, 1997.

Web Sites

Knight, Kevin. "Philip II." *Catholic Encyclopedia*. [Online] Available http://www.newadvent.org/cathen/12002a.htm, April 5, 2002.

Letters of Philip II, King of Spain, 1592–1597. [Online] Available http://library.byu.edu/~rdh/phil2/, April 5, 2002.

"Philip II." *Infoplease.com*. [Online] Available http://www.infoplease.com/ce5/CE040637.html, April 5, 2002.

François Rabelais

c. 1494
Chinon, France
1553
Chinon, France?

French humanist, physician, and prose satirist

"It is quite a common and vulgar thing among humans to understand, foresee, know and predict the troubles of others. But oh what a rare thing it is to predict, know, foresee and understand one's own troubles."

François Rabelais as quoted in Bartlett's Quotations. *[Online] Available http://www.bartleby.com/66/45/45745.html, April 5, 2002.*

The French humanist, physician, and author François Rabelais is acclaimed as a comic genius. He published several works, but he is best known for *Gargantua and Pantagruel.*

Facts of early life unknown

Unfortunately, there are large gaps in information about Rabelais's life. Some records suggest he was born in 1483, but it is widely believed the true date was closer to 1494. Rabelais was the son of a well-established lawyer in the town of Chinon, in the province of Touraine, France. He may have had a scholastic education, which would explain his dislike for overly learned, self-important scholars, an opinion he expressed in his writings. (Scholasticism was the dominant philosophical movement within the Catholic Church from the ninth to the seventeenth centuries. Scholastic thinkers sought to combine the ideas of ancient Greek philosophers with Christian teachings.) It is possible that as early as 1510 or 1511 Rabelais was a novice (a person given probationary admittance into a religious community) at the nearby Franciscan monastery (a religious community founded by Saint Francis of Assisi) of La Baumette, where he would have received the traditional education in church Latin and scholasticism.

The first documentary evidence of Rabelais's life is a letter he wrote in 1521, after he had entered the Franciscan order and joined a group of humanist scholars. (Humanists were members of a literary and intellectual movement dedicated to the study of classical languages and culture, which started in Italy in the mid-1300s. Humanism is credited with initiating the Renaissance.) Rabelais was one of a growing number of European scholars who could read Greek. This ability was significant because texts studied by the scholastics were Latin translations of works originally written in Greek. Sixteenth-century humanists such as the Dutch scholar **Desiderius Erasmus** (1466–1536; see entry) were discovering numerous errors in Latin versions of many works, especially the New Testament (second part of the Bible, the Christian holy book). In the first of a series of conflicts between Rabelais and the faculty of theology (professors of religion) at the University of Paris, the Greek and Latin texts of Rabelais and his circle were seized in 1523. At that time the University of Paris was the center of Catholic learning in Europe, and the theology faculty decided which books could be read by scholars and students alike. Although the faculty eventually returned Rabelais's books, Rabelais quickly moved to the less restrictive Benedictine order (monastic communities following the rule of Saint Benedict). He entered the service of Abbot (head of the monastery) Geoffroy d'Estissac, later bishop of Maillezais, who would remain an important patron, or financial supporter of Rabelais.

In 1527 Rabelais left the Benedictine order and became a priest. At some point in the next three years he must have spent considerable time studying medicine, perhaps at the University of Paris. In 1530 he registered at Montpellier University and received a bachelor of medicine degree six weeks later. While he practiced medicine periodically and even performed a dissection of, or cutting apart, a body for the purposes of medical observation in 1537, Rabelais distinguished himself in the profession through his linguistic skills. Medical school course work relied heavily on Latin translations of works by the early Greek medical writers Hippocrates (460–370 B.C.) and Galen (A.D. 129–c. 199). With his knowledge of Greek, Rabelais produced editions of these ancient medical texts that were both accurate and free of excessive commentary. He followed the lead of Erasmus and the French humanist Guillaume Budé (1467–1540), who worked with both secular (nonreligious) and sacred texts. In 1531 Rabelais lectured on Hippocrates at Montpellier, citing the original Greek text. The following year he settled in Lyons as a physician at the Hôtel-Dieu (a hospital) and published a new edition of Hippocrates's *Aphorism.*

Publishes *Gargantua and Pantagruel*

In 1531 Rabelais also began a series of sham, or fake, almanacs titled *Pantagrueline Prognosticato,* which he mockingly dedicated to "fools and idle dreamers." An almanac was a publication that gave a forecast of events for the coming year on the basis of astrology, a science devoted to predicting the future according to the positions of the stars and planets. Soon after beginning the almanacs Rabelais attached himself to one of his most important patrons, Cardinal Jean du Belay (c.1492–1560), the bishop of Paris. Despite the support of du Bellay, Rabelais would spend the remainder of his life on the margins of political and financial stability. Having identified with religious and intellectual reformers, he constantly came under suspicion from the faculty of theology at the University of Paris and the ever-changing French monarchy (government headed by a single ruler, such as a king or queen).

In 1534 Rabelais accompanied du Bullay to Rome as his personal physician. Upon returning to France, Rabelais published *Gargantua,* the history and adventures of the giant Pantagruel. *Gargantua* was the first part (book) of the novel *Gargantua and Pantagruel.* For years Rabelais had neglected his duties as a monk (one who lives in or is a member of a monastery) without the permission of the church, and on a second trip to Rome he sought and received absolution, or forgiveness, for deserting his order. No longer a monk, Rabelais attained his advanced medical degree from Montpellier in 1537. He then supported himself through his medical practice, support from patrons, and the modest income he received from his popular writings. In 1543 *Gargantua and Pantagruel* was again condemned by the Paris faculty of theology, but two years later Rabelais received permission from the king to publish more tales of Pantagruel. A third installment appeared the following year. After a third and final trip to Rome, Rabelais was made curate (clergyman in charge of a parish) of two parishes from which he drew a modest income and finally achieved a fair degree of financial security. In 1552 book four of *Gargantua and Pantagruel* was published. Rabelais died the following year, on a date unknown and under unclear circumstances.

An illustration from François Rabelais's *Garagantua and Pantagruel.* ©*Leonardo de Selva/Corbis. Reproduced by permission of Corbis Corporation.*

Garagantua and Pantagruel: political commentary through satire

Gargantua and Pantagruel consists of a collection of four books released separately, and out of sequence, over a period of twenty years (1532–52); a fifth book was published in two parts (1562 and 1564) after Rabelais's death. Scholars are still disputing whether he wrote Book Five, as it was published under the pseudonym, or pen name, Master Alcofibras, which contains the letters of Rabelais's name.

Rabelais based *Pantagruel* (book two) on a popular collection of fanciful French tales about giants, set against a background of the Arthurian legend (medieval stories about the legendary English hero King Arthur). These tales were called *Les grands et insetimables chroniques du géant Gargantua* (Chronicles of Gargantua). Rabelais presented his own work as a sequel to the tales. He depicted the birth, education, and adventures of Gargantua and his son Pantagruel, both of whom are giants. Two other characters play prominent roles in the stories. In *Gargantua* (book one), Friar Jean represents a new type of monk, a worldly and dynamic one, who tills the earth and performs heroic feats against the army attacking his vineyards. In *Pantagruel* (book two), Panurge is a comic prankster who becomes Pantagruel's companion. Scholars suggest that the birth and the military exploits of the giants in both *Gargantua* and *Pantagruel* gave Rabelais the opportunity to support Christian humanism and the Protestant reform movement. The author was also influenced by classical writers of a literary form called Menippean satire, which is a loose collection of parodies, or comic imitations, of intellectual and religious figures.

In book three, published fourteen years later, Rabelais abandoned both the chronicle (history) structure and the theme of Gargantua and Pantagruel battling with other giants. Pantagruel and Panurge consult a series of religious oracles (people who can predict the future) and professional experts to determine if Panurge should get married. Books four and five tell of the mock epic voyage (long, trouble-filled sea journey made in a quest for truth) undertaken by Pantagruel and Panurge to meet the oracle of the bottle, from whom they hope to discover the final answer to their question.

Rabelais wrote *Gargantua and Pantagruel* during a period of religious and intellectual turmoil in Europe. The Protestant Reformation, with its emphasis on individual faith without the intervention of priests and church officials, was a serious challenge to traditional beliefs. Religious unrest and social conflict were met by opposition from the French monarchy. The genius of Rabelais's work is that he was able to criticize the church by using satire through a mixture of intellectual, religious, and common language. Some scenes are funny because they are so ridiculous, while others are shocking in their denunciation of church officials, intellectuals, and royals. For instance, in one scene a pompous English scholar seeks a debate in which only hand signals can be used, since he contends words cannot possibly penetrate the mysteries of truth. Panurge responds with a series of indecent gestures used to mock the learned fool Thaumaste (see accompanying box).

Gargantua and Pantagruel also contains harsh challenges to the church as an institution. The work was repeatedly condemned by the Paris theologians, but this did little to prevent it from becoming popular. Scholars note that *Gargantua and Pantagruel* most certainly influenced *Don Quixote,* the

Thaumaste Versus Panurge

In book two, chapter nineteen of *Gargantua and Pantagruel,* the giant Pantagruel's closest friend, Panurge, enters into a "debate" with the English scholar Thaumaste on behalf of Pantagruel. Unlike traditional debates in which each participant voices his or her argument in an agreed-upon language, Thaumaste and Panurge attempt to penetrate the Inner Mysteries of truth by using only hand signals. After agreeing upon the rules in chapter eighteen, Panurge and Thaumaste begin their argument in chapter nineteen. The following is a brief excerpt from the scene.

> Then, with everyone attending and listening in perfect silence, the Englishman raised his two hands separately in the air, clenching all the tips of his fingers in the form that is known in the language of Chinon as the hen's arse, and struck the nails of one against the other four times. Then he opened them and struck the one with the flat of the other, making a sharp noise. Next, clenching them again, as before, he struck twice more and, after opening them, yet another four times. Then he joined them afresh and laid them one beside the other, as if offering up devout prayers to God.
>
> Suddenly Panurge lifted his right hand in the air, and placed his thumb inside his right nostril, holding his four fingers stretched out and arranged in their natural order, parallel to the tip of his nose, shutting his left eye entirely and winking with the right, at the same time deeply depressing his eyebrows and lids. Then he raised his left hand, widely stretching and extending his four fingers and elevating the thumb, and held it in line directly continuous with that of the right, the distance between the two being two and a quarter feet. This done, he lowered both hands towards the ground in this same attitude, and finally held them half way up, as if aimed straight at the Englishman's nose.

The scene continues, with each exchange of hand gestures getting more ridiculous and obscene. Finally, Panurge is declared the winner by Thaumaste in chapter twenty. For Rabelais the purpose of this exchange was to ridicule the scholastic methods used by the church to interpret the Scriptures, or text of the Bible. By having Panurge show a perfect understanding of philosophy and truth through seemingly incomprehensible hand gestures, Rabelais is able to make his point without specifically saying what he means. This method of satire was used by many humanists, most notably Erasmus, in attempts to ensure their safety from the wrath of the Catholic Church and the Holy Roman Empire.

Source: Rabelais, François. Gargantua and Pantagruel. J. M. Cohen, translator. New York: Viking Penguin, 1976, p. 234.

novel by Spanish author **Miguel de Cervantes** (1547–1616; see entry). Rabelais also had an impact on modern writers, and the adjective "Rabelaisian" has come to mean any text that is characterized by extravagant and coarse humor.

For More Information

Books

Rabelais, François. *Gargantua and Pantagruel.* J. M. Cohen, translator. New York: Viking Penguin, 1976.

Web Sites

"François Rabelais." *Bartlett's Quotations.* [Online] Available http://www.bartleby.com/66/45/45745.html, April 5, 2002.

"Rabelais, François." *Encyclopedia.com.* [Online] Available http://www.encyclopedia.com/searchpool.asp?target=francois+rabelais&Submit.x=29&Submit.y=16, April 5, 2002.

"Rabelais, François." *Informationplease.com.* [Online] Available http://www.infoplease.com/ce6/people/A0840877.html, April 5, 2002.

Raphael

April 6, 1483
Urbino, Italy
April 6, 1520
Rome, Italy

Painter, architect

The Italian painter and architect Raffaello Sanzio, called Raphael, is considered the supreme representative of the High Renaissance (1495–1520). This was the period when artistic expression reached its height in Italy, home of the Renaissance. Since the Renaissance began in the early 1400s, art had been based on concepts from classical, or ancient, Greek and Roman culture. Paintings were characterized by balanced proportions (harmonious arrangement of shapes and details), idealized images, and rich colors. Renaissance artists gave particular attention to achieving a sense of depth, or three dimensions, by using a technique called linear perspective. Invented by the Italian architect Filippo Brunelleschi (1377–1446), linear perspective is a system derived from mathematics in which all elements of a composition are measured and arranged from a single point of view, or perspective.

Moves to Florence

Raphael was born in Urbino, the son of Giovanni Santi, a painter. He was trained by his father, who died in

1494. Sometime thereafter Raphael joined the workshop of Perugino (Pietro Vannucci; c. 1450–1523), the most renowned painter in central Italy at the time. Raphael adopted Perugino's style and received several commissions. During his four years with Perugino, Raphael showed a remarkable ability to adapt borrowed ideas within a very personal style. Many works of this period, such as the *Mond Crucifixion* (1503), are in stylistic detail almost indistinguishable from Perugino's gentle technique, but they have a clarity and harmony that are lacking in Perugino's work. Raphael's last painting before leaving Perugino was *Marriage of the Virgin* (1504). It is primarily modeled on Perugino's version of the same subject. Raphael's design, however, has a greater sense of space and the figures are portrayed more accurately. Raphael also communicated the dramatic significance of the subject without the artificiality of pose and gesture seen in Perugino's work.

In 1504 Raphael moved to Florence, the center of Renaissance art. When he arrived he discovered that his style was unsophisticated compared with the recent innovations of the great Florentine painters **Michelangelo** (1475–1564; see entry) and **Leonardo** (1452–1519; see entry). Raphael was especially attracted to Leonardo's work. During the next four years he painted a series of Madonnas (pictures of Mary, mother of Jesus Christ) that incorporated Leonardo's techniques. One technique was sfumato, which involves defining a form by blending one color into another rather than using distinct outlines. It was principally, however, Michelangelo's *Battle of Cascina* rather than Leonardo's companion piece, the *Battle of Anghiari,* that provided the dramatic ideas used by Raphael in his most ambitious Florentine work, the *Entombment* (1507). During his stay in Florence he was also commissioned to do several portraits.

Paints *School of Athens*
In 1508 Raphael went to Rome to decorate the apartment of Pope Julius II (1433–1516; reigned 1503–13), the Stanza della Segnatura, at the Vatican (residence of the pope, who is the supreme head of the Roman Catholic Church). This work, which Raphael completed in 1511, con-

Raphael's architecture

In addition to achieving fame as a painter, Raphael was an architect. In 1509 he began working with Donato di Pascuccio d'Antonio (called Bramante; 1444–1514), the first influential Renaissance architect. Art historians speculate that Raphael was preparing to take over the post of *capomastro* (supervisor) of the rebuilding of Saint Peter's Basilica, the main church of the Roman Catholic faith, in Rome. Bramante died in 1514 and Raphael became *capomastro,* but progress on Saint Peter's was very slow during the next six years. Raphael's only contribution seems to have been suggesting the addition of a nave, or main part of a church to Bramante's design.

Raphael's first architectural work was the Saint Eligio degli Orefici church in Rome, which he designed in collaboration with Bramante in 1509. The building that more clearly shows Raphael's ornate decorative style is the Chigi Chapel in Saint Maria del Popolo (1513), also located in Rome. A similar emphasis on richness of texture and detailing can be seen in Raphael's two Roman palaces, the Palazzo Vidoni-Caffarelli and the Palazzo Branconio dell'Aquila (c.1520), both of which were destroyed. As in his last paintings, Raphael was moving away from the simple lines and shapes of Renaissance architecture to the more elaborate style of mannerism (the term given to the more expressive art of the sixteenth century).

sists of panels that represent the four areas of divinely inspired human intellect: theology (the study of religion), poetry, philosophy (the search for a general understanding of values and reality through speculative thinking), and law. The panel on philosophy, titled *The School of Athens,* is considered one of Raphael's greatest achievements. The two central figures are the ancient Greek philosophers Plato (c. 428–348 B.C.) and Aristotle (384–322 B.C.). As an idealist (one who believes that ultimate truth exists outside nature) Plato points heavenward, and the realist (one who finds truth in the known world) Aristotle gestures toward the ground. Around them are grouped many other classical philosophers and scientists, each indicating clearly by expression and gesture the character of his intellect. Raphael's painting technique is so precise that every detail in the *School of Athens* contributes to a balanced effect and conveys a sense of quiet grandeur.

Oversees productive workshop

After Raphael completed the Stanza della Segnatura, Julius commissioned him to decorate the adjacent room, the Stanza d' Elidoro (the audience chamber). Julius died before it was finished, but his successor, Pope Leo X (1475–1521; reigned 1513–21), told Raphael to continue. The pope eventually assigned him two more rooms, the Stanza dell' Incendio (the meeting room of the Catholic Church's supreme court) and the Sala di Constantino. Very quickly, Raphael became popular with Roman patrons, or wealthy supporters of the arts. Commissions of all sorts poured into his workshop during the last six years of his life. By this time he was relying on assistants. For instance, frescoes (wall paintings) in the Stanza dell'Incendio (1514–17) were based on his design but executed almost entirely by assistants, as was the fresco decoration of the Vatican loggias, or porches (1517–19). Many of his assistants were more collaborators (artists who produce works with other artists) than apprentices (beginning artists who learn from a master artist), and some were older than he. In 1515 he had what was probably the largest painting workshop that had ever been assembled. Reportedly, fifty artists accompanied Raphael daily to the Vatican.

Raphael also was much in demand by aristocrats (members of the upper social class) who wanted him to paint their portraits. In 1517 Raphael painted one of his best-known portraits, that of **Baldassare Castiglione** (1478–1529; see entry), author of the popular *Book of the Courtier*. Like most of Raphael's finest portraits, it is the depiction of a close friend. Castiglione is portrayed with great psychological insight, his gentle, scholarly face perfectly suited to the man, who in *Book of the Courtier* defined the qualities of the ideal gentleman. Descriptions of Raphael's own pleasant disposition and courteous manner indicate that he himself possessed the qualities Castiglione wished to find in the perfect courtier.

Capitalizes on art market

Raphael had by now developed his own style, which consisted of a distinctive use of color and an emphasis on gesture and movement. This style is evident is such works as the cartoons that depict the lives of two early church fathers,

Titian

Another important painter working at the same time as Raphael was Titian (Tiziano Vecellio; c. 1488–1576). Titian was born in Pieve di Cadore, Italy. He achieved fame as an interpreter of classical mythology with three paintings—*Andrians, Worship of Venus,* and *Bacchus and Ariadne*—which he composed for Alfonso d'Este's castle in Ferrara between 1518 and 1523. One of his best-known early works is the *Assumption of the Virgin* (1516–18), which marked the triumph of the High Renaissance in Venice. During the 1520s Titian produced the *Pesaro Madonna* (1519–26), in which he used color, light, and atmosphere to establish a new formula for Venetian altars that continued into the following century.

An important event in Titian's career was his trip to Bologna in 1530 to attend the coronation of Holy Roman Emperor Charles V (1500–1558). At this time the artist painted his first portrait of the emperor in armor. In 1545 Titian traveled to Rome, and saw the glories of the ancient city as well as the masterpieces of Raphael and Michelangelo. Among the numerous works he produced during his brief stay in Rome was *Paul III and His Grandsons,* which depicts a dramatic encounter between the aged pope and his scheming grandsons. It is considered one of the most psychologically revealing works in the history of portraiture. In 1548 Charles V called Titian to Augsburg, Germany. The artist painted the celebrated equestrian portrait, *Charles V at Mühlberg,* which commemorated the emperor's victory over the German Protestants in the Battle of Mühlberg in 1547. In this work Titian established a type of equestrian portrait that presents the ruler as a symbol of power. Titian also produced portraits of members of the emperor's court. The most important is that of Charles's son, Prince Philip (1527–1598), dressed in armor, which set a standard for state portraits. The prince later became Philip II, king of Spain. In the 1550s Philip II commissioned Titian to paint religious pictures for the monastery (a house for monks, members of a religious order) of the Escorial, the royal palace in Spain. Among them was the *Last Supper* (1557–64). During the same period Titian also executed mythological works for the Escorial, such as the *Rape of Europa.* Titian continued to explore the depths of human character in his portraits until the end of his life. His late religious pictures convey a mood of universal tragedy, as in the *Annunciation* (c.1565) and the *Christ Crowned with Thorns.* The *Pietà* which was unfinished at his death, was intended for his own tomb chapel. When Titian died at his spacious palace in Venice, he was universally recognized as one of the great masters.

Raphael's largest canvas painting, the *Transfiguration*. *Reproduced by permission of AP/Wide World Photos.*

Saints Peter and Paul. (At that time a cartoon had not yet come to mean a satirical or humorous drawing. Instead, it was a preparatory design or drawing for a fresco.) Other typical works were the decoration (begun 1519) of the Villa Farnesina in Rome and Raphael's largest canvas painting, the *Transfiguration*, which was commissioned in 1517 but remained incomplete at his death. The Peter and Paul cartoons were sent to Flanders to be worked into tapestries (large embroidered wall hangings) for the Sistine Chapel in the Vatican and were partly responsible for the adoption of Raphael's style throughout Europe. His work was also spread through engravings, or images made by printing from etched steel plates. The market for art prints was just then getting established and Raphael was one of the first to take advantages of it. Raphael supplied unused drawings and designs to engravers, who were required to follow his instructions regarding the production of images. He collaborated with the engraver Marcantonio Raimondi (c. 1480–c. 1534) and then allied himself with a businessman known as Il Bavieri, who was responsible for selling the engravings. Raphael appears to have set certain conditions with engravers to control quality and his copyright (exclusive legal right to the sale and reproduction of a work), and he received most of the profits for these engravings.

When Raphael died in Rome at age thirty-seven his art was developing in new directions. The High Renaissance, which had reached its peak around 1510, had passed. Raphael's pupils began incorporating characteristics of the mannerist style in the last works of their great master. Raphael had made major contributions to painting. He invented new modes of composing a picture and new techniques for using color, which were often imitated.

Raphael was a master of linear perspective, which was evolving throughout the High Renaissance. He also invented the concept of modes of coloring, in that he was the first to select a color style to match a project. This was an innovation because, in the traditional workshop of the fifteenth century, a master typically had only one color style, which he taught to his apprentices. As a result of Raphael's experimentations with color, the next generation of painters felt liberated to vary their choice of colors with each commission and to develop new modes.

Raphael's reputation suffered in the twentieth century because his style had been adopted as the model for academic art, beginning in the French Academy of the sixteenth century. Elements of his methods were taught to young painters as strict rules. This practice contradicted the freedom that Raphael allowed his own students and collaborators. It was also inconsistent with his experimental approach, in which he never repeated himself. Nevertheless, Raphael has been recognized as one of the greatest European painters, not only of the Renaissance but of all time.

For More Information

Books

Cole, Bruce. *Titian and Venetian Painting, 1450–1590.* Boulder, Colo.: Icon Editions/Westview Press, 1999.

Cuzin, Jean-Pierre. *Raphael: His Life and Works.* Secaucus, N.J.: Chartwell Books, 1985.

Mühlberger, Richard. *What makes a Raphael a Raphael?* New York: Viking, 1993.

Venezia, Mike. *Raphael.* New York: Children's Press, 2001.

Video Recordings

Masterpieces of Italian Art, Volume: Da Vinci, Michelangelo, Raphael and Titian. New York: VPI-AC Video Inc., 1990.

Web Sites

Pioch, Nicolas. "Raphael." *WebMuseum.* [Online] Available http://sunsite. unc.edu/wm/paint/auth/raphael, April 5, 2002.

Pioch, Nicolas. "Vecellio, Tiziano—Titian." *WebMuseum.* http://sunsite. unc.edu/wm/paint/auth/titian/, April 5, 2002.

"Raphael." *MSN Encarta.* [Online] Available http://encarta.msn.com/ find/Concise.asp?z=1&pg=2&ti=761570572, April 5, 2002.

"Raphael, Sanzio." *Raphael, Stanza e Loggia.* [Online] Available http:// www.christusrex.org/www1/stanzas/0-Raphael.html, April 5, 2002.

Peter Paul Rubens

June 28, 1577
Siegen, Westphalia, Germany
May 30, 1640
Antwerp, Belgium

Painter, diplomat

The Flemish painter and diplomat (one who conducts negotiations between governments) Peter Paul Rubens was one of the best-known artists of the seventeenth century. He received commissions from Italy, Spain, France, England, and Germany as well as from his homeland, the southern Netherlands. His boundless imagination, capacity for work, and productivity were legendary during his lifetime. In 1621, when he was not yet forty-five years old, an English visitor to Antwerp (a city in present-day Belgium) described him as "the master workman of the world." Rubens said of himself, without boasting, that his talent was so great that no other artist could equal him in the variety of subjects he painted and the number of works he produced. Without interrupting his artistic activity, he also had a demanding career as a diplomat. Rubens is considered the master of a style of painting called baroque, which was characterized by large, dramatic works in deep colors and hues (see accompanying box). Although the baroque period came at the end of the Renaissance, Rubens's work is considered the culmination of Italian Renaissance art.

"My talent is such that no enterprise, however vast in number and in diversity of subjects, has surpassed my courage."

Peter Paul Rubens.

Peter Paul Rubens.
©Bettmann/Corbis.
Reproduced by permission of Corbis Corporation.

Rubens was born in 1577 in Siegen, Westphalia, Germany. His father, Jan Rubens, had been a lawyer in Antwerp (a city in present-day Belgium) before fleeing to Cologne, Germany, in 1568 because he was a Calvinist. Calvinists were members of a religious group that followed the teachings of the Protestant reformer **John Calvin** (1509–1564; see entry). At that time the Low Countries (present-day Belgium, Luxembourg, the Netherlands, and parts of northern France) were ruled by Spain, a Catholic nation. In Cologne Jan Rubens entered into an adulterous relationship with the wife of William I (called the Silent; 1533–1584), Prince of Orange. As a result Jan Rubens was thrown into prison. He was released two years later through the efforts of his wife, Maria Pypelinckx, and permitted to go to Siegen. The family, who had now become Catholic, lived in Cologne until Jan Rubens died in 1587. His widow returned to Antwerp, taking her three children with her.

Starts painting career in Rome

Peter Paul Rubens received a classical education, which included instruction in Latin and Greek. He then became a page, or court attendant, to a noblewoman, Marguerite de Ligne, countess of Lalaing. This early experience of court life was undoubtedly useful to the future artist, who later spent much of his time in aristocratic and royal circles. After returning to Antwerp, Rubens decided to follow the profession of painter. He studied under three masters (supervisors)—Tobias Verhaecht, Adam van Noort, and Otto van Veen—and in 1598 he was accepted as a master painter into Antwerp's Guild of Saint Luke, a professional organization for artists and craftsmen.

In 1600 Rubens went to Italy, where he entered the service of Vincenzo Gonzaga (1562–1612), duke of Mantua, whose palace housed a notable art collection. Since Rubens was not expected to spend all of his time at the duke's court, he found time to visit other cities in Italy, especially Rome, Florence, and Genoa. In Rome he completed his education as an artist, studying the sculptures of antiquity and the paintings of the High Renaissance, especially those of **Raphael** (1483–1520; see entry) and **Michelangelo** (1475–1564; see entry). During his stay in Rome, from 1601 until 1602, he painted three altarpieces (works of art that decorate an altar for the Church) of Saint Croce in Gerusalemme. In 1603 Gonzaga sent Rubens on a diplomatic mission to Spain. Here he made the impressive equestrian (rider mounted on a horse) portrait of the Duke of Lerma. Rubens also saw for the first time the art collection that Spanish king Philip I (1478–1506) had assembled at El Escorial, the royal palace. Included in the collection were numerous paintings by the Italian master Titian.

When Rubens returned to Rome again in 1605 he managed to remain there for almost three years. During this time he was commissioned to decorate the high altar of San Maria in Vallicella, an unusual honor for a foreigner. For this project he painted an altarpiece showing the Madonna and Child (Mary and the infant Jesus) with Saint Gregory (early pope and Christian scholar; c. 540–604) and other saints. This work did not make a good impression because the lighting conditions in the church were unfavorable. Rubens then made a set of three pictures painted on slate. In 1608, before this work had been unveiled, he received word that his mother was seriously ill. Upon reaching Antwerp he learned that she had already died. Although Rubens planned to return to Italy, he soon found reasons for remaining in Antwerp. The rulers of the Spanish Netherlands, Archduke Albert VII (1559–1621) and Duchess Isabella, appointed him court painter with special privileges. In 1609 Rubens married Isabella Brant, and a year later he purchased a house in Antwerp. Around this time he painted *Rubens and His Wife in the Honeysuckle Arbor.*

The baroque period

The "baroque period" is generally used to describe the music, art, literature, and philosophy of the seventeenth century. The concept of the baroque emerged in the eighteenth century to describe an exuberant, sensuous, expressive, and dynamic style that was different from the classical style of the Renaissance. For advocates of Renaissance ideals, this era was an age of decadence, or decline. Its manners, morals, and arts were absurd, grotesque, corrupt, and contrary to good (that is, classical) principles. The word "baroque" may have come from the Portuguese *barroco* and the Spanish *barrueco,* terms for a misshapen pearl. Another origin may have been a nonsensical word created by medieval logicians (scholars who study logic, or the use of reason in thinking) for a convoluted, or excessively complicated, argument. Whatever the origin of the word, the eighteenth century carried on its negative connotations to condemn the baroque for not being the Renaissance.

Produces two thousand paintings

The first major project Rubens undertook after returning from Italy was *Raising of the Cross* (1611), a triptych (three-panel painting) for the church of Saint Walburga. With this bold and dramatic work Rubens established himself as the leading master of the city. It was followed by an equally large triptych, *Descent from the Cross* (1614), in the cathedral in Antwerp. Rubens's imagination found new outlets in subjects from both the sacred and secular (nonreligious) worlds. In *The Last Judgment* (c. 1616) he portrayed an apocalyptic vision (warning of impending disaster) of the torments of the damned, or sinners. The same tempestuous, or stormy, energy can be seen in the artist's hunting pieces, with their ferocious combats of men and wild beasts.

Rubens's workshop was now in full operation. With the aid of his pupils and assistants, he achieved an astonishing output of pictures—more than two thousand paintings have been attributed to his studio. The most brilliant of these assistants was Anthony Van Dyck (1599–1641), who joined Rubens's workshop in 1617 or 1618 and helped in the execution of a number of important commissions. Nevertheless, Rubens was not simply content to let his assistants do all the work. The paintings coming from his studio were of the highest quality, indicating that the artist himself was involved in producing them. Indeed there were so many masterpieces at this time that it is difficult to select a few representative examples. One of his most dazzling works on a mythological subject is *Rape of the Daughters of Leucippus*. Among his finest religious works are two altarpieces glorifying the **Ignatius of Loyola** (c. 1491–1556; see entry) and Francis Xavier (1506–1552), the first saints of Jesuit, or Society of Jesus, order. Titled *Miracles of St. Ignatius of Loyola* and *Miracles of St. Francis Xavier,* these huge paintings feature a richness of color and depth of feeling that nearly overwhelm the observer.

The Jesuit altarpieces were followed by an even larger commission from France. In 1622 Rubens went to Paris to decorate two great galleries in the Luxembourg Palace, the residence of the queen mother, Marie de Médicis (1573–1642). The first of these projects, a series of twenty-one large canvases illustrating the life of Marie, was completed in 1625. Rubens succeeded in transforming the uninspiring story of the queen's life into one of the most brilliant and spectacular of all baroque decorative projects. Rubens had other commissions during this period. For King Louis XIII (1601–1643; ruled 1610–43) of France he designed the tapestry series *History of Constantine the Great.* Several years later he designed an even larger tapestry cycle, *Triumph of the Eucharist,* for the Convent of the Descalzas Reales in Madrid, Spain.

Rubens also painted important altarpieces for churches in Antwerp. *Adoration of the Magi* (1624) was made for Saint Michael's Abbey; *Assumption of the Virgin* (1626) for the high altar of the cathedral; and perhaps the most beautiful of all, *Madonna and Saints* (sometimes called *Mystic Marriage of St. Catherine;* 1628) for the church of the Augustinians (a religious order). Rubens painted some of his most memorable portraits during these years. Hanging in Windsor Castle in England is his famous *Self-portrait* (1624), which he painted at the request of the Prince of Wales, later King Charles I (1600–1649; ruled 1625–49) of England. It shows the strong and handsome face of the artist, with a bold moustache and curling hair and beard. He is wearing a broad-brimmed hat that not only lends interest to the picture but serves also to conceal his baldness, about which he seems to have been rather sensitive.

Peter Paul Rubens's painting *Descent from the Cross* found in the cathedral in Antwerp. *©World Films Enterprise/Corbis. Reproduced by permission of Corbis Corporation.*

Succeeds as diplomat

Rubens's diplomatic activity had begun some time earlier. It reached a peak in the years between 1628 and 1630, when he was instrumental in bringing about peace between England and Spain. In addition to carrying out his political duties he found a new and enthusiastic patron (financial supporter) in the Spanish king, Philip IV (1605–1665; ruled 1621–65), who knighted him in 1631. Rubens's mission to

England was equally successful. Charles I knighted him artist-diplomat, and the University of Cambridge awarded him an honorary master of arts degree. Rubens returned to Antwerp in 1630. That year he married Helena Fourment, a girl of sixteen. His first wife, Isabella Brant, had died four years earlier. Though he had hoped to withdraw from political life, he was a confidential agent for Spain in the frustrating and unsuccessful negotiations with the Dutch, who were seeking independence. Finally he retired from his diplomatic career, and in 1635 he purchased a country estate, the Castle of Steen, south of Antwerp. In the last decade of his life Rubens expanded the subject matter of his art. An example is *Garden of Love,* (1623) a complex interweaving of classical and contemporary themes. He expressed a new interest in nature, inspired perhaps by his residence in the country. He painted a series of magnificent landscapes, among them *Castle of Steen.* The portraits of this period, especially those of his wife Helena and their children, are characterized by informality and tender intimacy.

During this period Rubens communicated a lyrical, or poetic, quality in his depictions of Christian and classical subjects. For instance, in the *Ildefonso Altarpiece* the scene of a saint receiving a vestment (religious garment) from Mary shimmers with a silvery radiance. The secular counterpart to this work is *Feast of Venus,* in which Rubens paid tribute both to the art of antiquity and to the paintings of Titian. The almost dreamlike poetry of his mythological subjects is exemplified by *Judgment of Paris* and *Three Graces,* in which opulent nude figures seem to glow with light and color. Rubens continued to carry out monumental commissions during his last decade. For Charles I of England he executed the ceiling paintings of the Banqueting House at Whitehall, which is a glorification of the reign of **James I** (1566–1625; see entry) and the Stuart monarchy. It is the only large-scale decorative work by the artist that still remains in the place for which it was designed. In 1635 the new governor of the Netherlands, Duchess Isabella's nephew Cardinal Infante Ferdinand, arrived in Antwerp. An elaborate celebration was held in the governor's honor, and Rubens was given the task of preparing the temporary street decorations. Swiftly mobilizing teams of artists and craftsmen to work from his designs, he created an elaborate series of painted theaters and triumphal arches that surpassed all expectations by their magnificence. His last great project was a vast cycle of mythological paintings for the decoration of Philip IV's hunting lodge near Madrid, the Torre de la Parada. Toward the end of his life Rubens was increasingly troubled by arthritis (inflammation of the joints), which eventually compelled him to give up painting altogether. He died in Antwerp in 1640.

For More Information

Books

Fletcher, Jennifer. *Peter Paul Rubens; With Fifty Plates in Full Colour*. New York: Phaidon, 1968.

McLanathan, Richard. *Peter Paul Rubens*. New York: H.N. Abrams, 1995.

Wedgwood, Cicely V. and the editors of Time-Life Books. *The World of Rubens, 1577-1640*. New York: Time-Life, Inc., 1967.

Web Sites

Howe, Jeffery. "House of Peter Paul Rubens." *A Digital Archive of Architecture*. [Online] Available http://www.bc.edu/bc_org/avp/cas/fnart/arch/rubens_arch.html, April 5, 2002.

Pioch, Nicolas. "Rubens, Peter Paul." *WebMuseum*. [Online] Available http://sunsite.unc.edu/wm/paint/auth/rubens/, December 10, 2001.

"Rubens, Peter Paul." *National Gallery of Art*. [Online] Available http://www.nga.gov/collection/gallery/gg45/gg45-main1.html, April 5, 2002.

Girolamo Savonarola

1452
Ferrara, Italy
May 23, 1498
Florence, Italy

Preacher, reformer

Girolamo Savonarola.
Photograph courtesy of The Library of Congress.

The Italian preacher and reformer Girolamo Savonarola was one of the most distinctive figures of the Renaissance. The Renaissance was a cultural movement which began in Italy in the mid-1300s. It was initiated by scholars called humanists who promoted the human-centered values of ancient Greece and Rome. Humanist ideals were soon influencing the arts, literature, philosophy, science, religion, and politics in Italy. Claiming the gift of prophecy, the mendicant monk (member of a religious order dedicated to a life of poverty) rose to power in Florence, Italy, through his harsh criticism of the Roman Catholic Church. He was angered by the corrupt behavior of popes, cardinals, and bishops. He demanded stricter adherence to the spiritual values of Christianity and greater social awareness of the poor. Earning the title, "Preacher of the Despairing," Savonarola gave immensely popular sermons (religious speeches on proper moral conduct) and became famous for his visions. His first vision was about the "Scourge [whip] of the Church," which would come to banish the evil materialism of the Catholic clergy. He also correctly predicted the deaths of **Lorenzo de' Medici** (1449–1492; see entry), the powerful duke of Florence, and

Pope Innocent VIII (1432–1492; reigned 1484–92), who both died in 1492.

Becomes popular preacher

Savonarola was born in Ferrara, Italy, the son of a banker. His grandfather, Michele Savonarola, was a noted physician and medical writer. After receiving a humanistic education (a curriculum based on study of ancient Greek and Latin literary texts), Girolamo earned a master's degree and studied medicine. In 1475 he entered the monastery of San Domenico in Bologna, Italy. He vowed to become a champion of Christ and battle human misery and sin. He studied theology (theory of religion) until 1482, when he was assigned to San Marco, a monastery in Florence. He began to preach on such themes as sin, God's punishment, and Christ's redeeming love. Savonarola was unsuccessful at first because his voice and accent annoyed the cultured citizens of Florence, who found his sermons boring. Away from Florence, however, his preaching was more dramatic. Savonarola served for three years at a monastery in Bologna before returning to San Marco in 1490.

Around 1491 Savonarola was named prior (second in rank to the abbot, or head, of a monastery) of San Marco. By now his preaching had become immensely popular, not only with the common people but also with the leading intellectuals and artists in Lorenzo de' Medici's circle. They flocked around him, many describing themselves as spellbound by his eloquence. They were convinced that his sermons were divinely inspired, that is, he was speaking the word of God. Well-born ladies and gentlemen also attended his sermons and pressed him for private attention. Savonarola's sermons reached a peak during Advent (a period beginning four Sundays before Christmas) in 1492, when he prophesied the coming of the "Scourge of Italy." This vision may have been prompted by the election of the new pope (supreme head of the Roman Catholic Church), **Alexander VI** (1431–1503; see entry), after the death of Innocent VIII. Alexander's behavior—taking mistresses, advancing members of his own family to prominent church positions, and squandering money on clothes and horses—was outrageous even in a time known for its corruption and decadence (decline). Savonarola set out to reform the church in Florence. His first step was to withdraw the monastery of San Marco from the Congregation of Lombardy, the ruling organization of monasteries in the region. He then formed a new, stricter congregation, Congregation of Tuscany (later renamed the Congregation of San Marco) which was approved by the pope in 1493. Savonarola saw the separation as the beginning of reform in the church. Expanding his movement, he convinced other monasteries to join his congregation. In his own monastery, he demanded that monks give up all possessions, which were then sold to raise money for the poor.

Initiates new government in Florence

Savonarola had also been criticizing the city government and was a bitter enemy of Lorenzo de' Medici before the duke's death. In 1494 Savonarola's prophecy of the "Scourge of Italy" was fulfilled when King Charles VIII (1470–1498; ruled 1483–98) of France invaded Italy in the first phase of the Italian Wars (a conflict between France and Spain over control of territory in Italy; 1494–1559). Lorenzo's son and the new duke of Florence, Piero de' Medici (1471–1503), fled from Italy and threw himself upon the mercy of the French king. The leading political body of Florence, the Signoria, elected Savonarola to ask Charles to insure Florence's security and safety but withdrawing his army from Florence. At first the king resisted Savonarola's request, but after extensive discussion the French army left Florence. Savonarola then turned to the problem of a new government without the Medicis. He proposed replacing the city's numerous councils with a single body modeled on the Maggior Consiglio (great council) in Venice. The new government, called the Consiglio Maggiore, was adopted in December 1494. It was the largest government Florence had ever had, with about three thousand members, all of them male. Savonarola hailed the new measure as the foundation of the *governo popolare,* or popular government, and claimed credit for it.

In his sermons Savonarola suggested new policies. For instance, he demanded an increase in jobs for the lower classes and relief for the poor. He also urged the churches to melt down their gold and silver ornaments to buy bread for the hungry. In 1495 he met resistance when a group called the *Tiepidi*

The "New Jerusalem"

Beginning in December 1494, when Florence adopted a new form of government, Girolamo Savonarola preached almost daily. He envisioned a city in which politics and religion were interrelated. He took credit for the fact that Florence was now safe and free, claiming this was evidence of his godly ministry and the city's divine election. Now Florentines must "reform their consciences," make good laws, and fulfill the city's destiny as the New Jerusalem (Jerusalem is the city in Palestine where Jesus Christ, lived and spread the teachings that are the basis of Christianity.) The fourth age of the world, the state of uninspired Christians, was ending, Savonarola said. The fifth age, of the Antichrist (enemy of Christ), was about to begin. In partnership with the crusader king, Charles VIII of France, Florence would lead the world out of the fifth age into the sixth and final age of universal Christianity and peace. "Spread your empire," he urged the Florentines, "and thus you will have power temporal [earthly] and spiritual."

Surrounded by zealous priests and lay followers—called Piagnoni, or wailers, by their enemies—Savonarola took his campaign directly to the people. He and his lieutenants gave frequent, intense sermons, rallying the city's riotous youth. They staged religious processions and organized the notorious "bonfires of the vanities," burning suggestive books and pictures, immodest clothing and female ornaments, and playing cards and dice—all considered dangerous to good morals.

(the lukewarm) was formed by priests, nuns, and monks who were opposed to strict observance of the vows of poverty and obedience. The Tiepidi received support from Pope Alexander, Duke Ludovico Sforza (1452–1508) of Milan, and Holy Roman Emperor Maximilian I (1459–1519; reigned 1493–1519), who had formed an alliance, called the Holy League, to oppose Charles VIII. The League needed backing from Florence, but first they had to remove Savonarola from power.

Challenged by pope

In 1495 Savonarola became ill with dysentery (an intestinal disease caused by an infection). Although his doctors told him to rest, he returned to the pulpit and delivered stinging sermons against his opponents, especially the Tiepidi. In response, Pope Alexander sent an official letter stating that certain people had accused Savonarola of committing heresy, or violation of the laws of the church, and false prophecy and troubling the peace of the church. Though he praised Savonarola's work, Alexander insisted that he come to Rome to defend himself. Since Savonarola was still weak from his illness, he asked permission to stay in Florence. The pope agreed, but told him to stop preaching until the accusations could be proven false. Over the next few months Savonarola's supporters continued to cause social and political unrest in Florence. The pope finally became angry about the situation and ordered Savonarola to stand trial. When an investigation found no evidence against Savonarola, Alexander canceled plans for a trial but would not lift the ban on preaching.

In 1496 the people of Florence persuaded the pope to allow Savonarola to preach sermons during Lent. (Lent is a forty-day period of fasting and prayer before Easter, the holy day commemorating Jesus's resurrection from the dead.) Once again Savonarola lashed out at the church, charging that abuses had gone beyond all bounds and that the clergy no longer observed their own rules. He met with opposition, however, when he demanded that the government pass stricter laws regulating the dress and ornamentation of Florentine women. By refusing to pass such a statute, city leaders took their first step away from Savonarola's reform platform. In 1497 new members of the Signoria who supported the Holy League began passing laws that limited Savonarola's preaching. On May 4, a gang of young aristocrats known as the Compagnacci (bad companions) started a riot while he was giving a sermon, apparently hoping to kill him. Though loyal monks saved his life, Florentine leaders identified him as the source of discontent in the city, and many demanded his exile. Alexander then excommunicated (expelled from the church) Savonarola and his followers for committing heresy. This event brought a deeper split among the Florentine factions, or opposing groups. In July the pope and his cardinals decided Savonarola must either come to Rome or abandon his reforms.

The final showdown between Savonarola and the pope began on February 11, 1498, when Alexander ordered the Signoria to silence the disobedient monk In April, Florentine officials conducted two three-day trials. During both trials they tortured and questioned Savonarola for evidence against him and two companions, Fra (Brother) Domenico da Pescia and Fra Silvestro Maruffi. Though Savonarola signed a confession, lack of sufficient evidence led to the second trial. With the verdict already decided, a two-day church trial then took place in May. The church court passed a death sentence for all three clergymen. On May 23, 1498, Savonarola and his two companions were hanged and their bodies were cremated, or burned. Government officials scattered the ashes in the Arno River to prevent the veneration (declaration of holiness) of the remains.

Outside Florence the interest in Savonarola's prophecy had been widespread. Venice was the major center for the publication of his sermons and writings. Savonarola's reputation as a spiritual leader and reformer grew steadily. His meditations, devotional literature, and religious ideas were translated into many European languages. His fervid commitment to Christian teachings was an important influence on the Spirituali, a group of sixteenth-century Catholic reformers. **Martin Luther** (1483–1546; see entry) and other Protestant reformers regarded him as a forerunner to their movement. In the eighteenth century Savonarola again became a symbol of liberation and spiritual rebirth in Europe. He was the subject of numerous historical dramas. In modern-day Italy a group of San Marco scholars, called the New Piagnoni, began collecting documents for the study of Savonarola's life and work. Other devotees are pressing for the withdrawal of his excommunication, the first step toward officially proclaiming him a saint.

For More Information

Books
De La Bedoyere, Michael. *The Meddlesome Friar and the Wayward Pope; The Story of the Conflict between Savonarola and Alexander VI.* Garden City, N.Y.: Hanover House, 1958.

Erlanger, Rachel. *The Unarmed Prophet: Savonarola in Florence.* New York: McGraw-Hill, 1988.

Web Sites
Knight, Kevin. "Girolamo Savonarola." *Catholic Encyclopedia.* [Online] Available http://www.newadvent.org/cathen/13490a.htm, April 5, 2002.

Kren, Emil, and Daniel Marx. *Portrait of Girolamo Savonarola by Bartolomeo, Fra.* [Online] Available http://www.kfki.hu/~arthp/html/b/bartolom/fra/savonaro.html, April 5, 2002.

"Savonarola, Girolamo." *MSN Encarta.* [Online] Available http://encarta.msn.com/index/conciseindex/4B/04BA3000.htm?z=1&pg=2&br=1, April 5, 2002.

William Shakespeare

April 23, 1564
Stratford-upon-Avon, England
April 23, 1616
Stratford-upon-Avon, England

Playwright, poet

The English playwright, poet, and actor William Shakespeare is generally considered the greatest of English writers and one of the most extraordinary creators in human history. The crucial fact about his career is that he was a popular dramatist at a time when drama (a composition in verse or prose depicting conflicts through dialogue) was flourishing in England. Audiences drawn from a wide range of social classes were eager to reward his talents. Shakespeare's entire life was committed to the public theater, and he seems to have written nondramatic poetry only when enforced closings of the theater made writing plays impractical. Perhaps his greatest achievement was the portrayal of the emotional states that are essential to human life, such as falling in love, knowing the need for friendship and loyalty, going through midlife crisis, growing old, and facing the approach of death. Possessing an unusual talent with words, he addressed the weighty issues of human existence in words that continue to enchant audiences and readers. Shakespeare is today the most quoted author in the English language.

"What a piece of work is man!... The beauty of the world, the paragon of animals! And yet, to me, what is this quintessence of dust?"

Hamlet, *Act 2, scene 2.*

William Shakespeare.
Reproduced by permission of AP/Wide World Photos.

wrote *Greene's Groatsworth of Wit Bought with a Million of Repentance* (1592), in which he warned fellow dramatists Christopher Marlowe (1564–1593), Thomas Nash (1567–1601), and George Peele (1556–1596) to beware of the ingratitude of a fickle public. He lashed out at a certain unnamed new playwright—easily identifiable as Shakespeare—whose plays were becoming more popular than those of established London playwrights. The reference to "Shake-scene" is a clue that the "upstart crow" was Shakespeare, whom Greene accused of gaining public favor by plagiarizing, or copying, works of the successful dramatists of the time—that is, beautifying himself with their feathers. Scholars note that Greene's attack was clearly the envious reaction of an older playwright dismayed at the appearance of a bright new star in the London theater world. By this time Shakespeare had written a few plays, and it is known that his historical play, *Henry VI*, had been a great hit, possibly as early as 1589. In fact, one line in *Henry VI* is "O tiger's heart wrapped in a woman's hide," which Greene repeated nearly verbatim, and another clue that he was targeting Shakespeare.

The incident over the charge of plagiarism not only confirms that Shakespeare was active in the London theatrical scene in 1592, but it also gives a character sketch of him. Greene's attack brought an apology from Henry Chettle (c. 1560–1607), a dramatist who had assisted in the printing of *Greene's Groatsworth of Wit*. Chettle published *Kind Heart's Dream* (1592), in which he insisted he had had no part in the matter. He went on to say that so fine a person as Shakespeare should not have been singled out for criticism. Chettle described Shakespeare as being courteous and an excellent playwright and actor. Furthermore, Shakespeare is judged to be upright by persons of social dignity and morality. A special talent is the great facility and swiftness with which he composed his works. All this, in Chettle's view, shows Shakespeare's honesty and his superior skills as a dramatist.

Shakespeare's earliest literary efforts were two nondramatic poems, *Venus and Adonis* (1593) and *Rape of Lucrece* (1594). They were published with dedications to Anthony Bacon, earl of Southampton, who may have been Shakespeare's patron, or financial supporter. Quite possibly Shakespeare wanted to be a nondramatic poet like Edmund Spenser

Edmund Spenser

Edmund Spenser (c. 1552–1599) ranks as the foremost English poet of the sixteenth century. His best-known work was the unfinished epic poem *The Faerie Queene.* (An epic poem is one that portrays events over a long period of time.) Along with William Shakespeare and Ben Jonson, he is considered one of the great figures of the English Renaissance. Spenser was working as a government official when he began writing poetry. He made his literary debut with *The Shepherd's Calendar* in 1579. In this work he adopted a variety of poetic forms—dirges, complaints, paeans—and attempted to enrich the English poetic vocabulary with foreign terms and archaic, or outdated, and dialect (distinctive to a region) words. The following year he was named secretary to Arthur Grey de Wilton (1536–1593), the new lord deputy of Ireland. Spenser moved to Ireland, where he remained for the rest of his life, except for brief trips to England.

In 1589 Spenser published the first three books of *The Faerie Queene,* with an elaborate dedication to Elizabeth I (1533–1603), queen of England. Spenser's plan was to compose twelve books, each concerned with one of the twelve moral virtues as classified by ancient Greek philosopher Aristotle (384–322 B.C.). In turn, each of these virtues was to be embodied in a knight. Spenser's style is distinctively his own in *The Faerie Queene.* For his verse form he created the Spenserian stanza, which has since often been imitated in English literature. Composed of nine lines, the Spenserian stanza contains eight lines of iambic pentameter (five metrical feet, or units of one syllable followed by one long syllable) and concludes with a line of iambic hexameter (six metrical feet, or units of one short syllable followed by one long syllable) called the Alexandrine. *The Faerie Queene* met with much acclaim.

In 1594 Spenser married Elizabeth Boyle. His sonnet series "Amoretti" and the love poem "Epithalamion" give a poetic account of his courtship and marriage. "Epithalamion" is regarded as one of the greatest love poems in English. Spenser published three more books of *The Faerie Queene* in 1595. Two cantos, or parts, of a seventh book were published in 1609, but most of what he wrote in the years before his death has been lost. Spenser died in London in 1598. He was buried near other poets in Westminster Abbey.

(c. 1552–1599; see accompanying box). For instance, writing poetry was more prestigious than playwriting. Also, he evidently cared enough about his early poems to personally tend to their publication, whereas he never bothered to have his plays printed.

Did he actually write the plays?

Since the nineteenth century, literary scholars have debated whether Shakespeare actually wrote the plays and poems attributed to him. Many note that he was a commoner without a university education, and he left no manuscripts or correspondence. Moreover, they argue, William Shakespeare of Stratford-upon-Avon may have been barely literate. The few signatures in his own handwriting—including the one on his last will and testament—are shaky, and his name is spelled in various ways. Therefore, could a country boy from Stratford, educated (if at all) only through what we would now call high school, have produced such brilliant studies of kings and aristocrats?

Many candidates have been put forward as the author of the plays. Those who present the case against Shakespeare are the anti-Stratfordians. They are given this title because they acknowledged that Shakespeare of Stratford did exist as an actor but they deny that he was a writer. The first candidate-of-choice of the anti-Stratfordians is the scientific theorist **Francis Bacon** (1561–1626; see entry). Others include Anthony Bacon, earl of Southampton; Charles Blout (c. 1562–1606), earl of Devonshire; Christopher Marlowe; and, most recently, Edward de Vere (1560–1604), seventeenth earl of Oxford. This last person has been a favorite candidate because he did in fact write verse, and he served for many years as a courtier, or member of court, under the queen of England, Elizabeth I. Oxford was also involved in various controversies that sound at times like plots from some of Shakespeare's plays. In addition, Oxford was the son-in-law of William Cecil (1520–1598), Lord Burghley, whom critics and scholars regard as a model for the character of Polonius in Shakespeare's famous tragedy *Hamlet*. Like Polonius, Burghley was a cautious, overly quarrelsome, and pompous statesman, or politician. A major problem with Oxford's being the true author, however, is that he died in 1604, before the dates that most scholars give to the chief plays of Shakespeare's later career.

One theory is that Oxford or one of the other candidates may have written the plays and then allowed Shakespeare to take credit for them. But why would these writers wish to see their great plays ascribed to an ordinary actor? The answer from the anti-Stratfordian side is that playwriting brought very little glory, much like script writing for the film industry or television today. It may have been profitable, but it was beneath the dignity of the English ruling class. Aristocrats and gentry of the time did indeed scorn commercial publication of the verses they turned out only as a pastime. Therefore, the argument goes, Oxford could have written the plays and then used Shakespeare as a "front man" in order to avoid the embarrassment of being associated with the theater world. One version of this view is that Oxford wanted to remain anonymous during his lifetime and then be revealed as the true author of the great plays centuries after his death. The problem with this argument is that a number of people would have had to participate secretly in such a complex endeavor—not only Oxford and Shakespeare himself but also others such as his fellow actors and Ben Jonson, who knew Shakespeare all his adult life.

Those who argue that Shakespeare was the true author raise several points in his defense. First, they say, it is necessary to consider whether university training and experience at court would have been necessary to enable him to write the plays and poems. They note that although English university education in the sixteenth century was directed mainly at preparing young men for the ministry, some professional writers of the Renaissance period did go to a university. (The Renaissance was a cultural revolution that began in Italy in the mid-1300s. It was initiated by scholars called humanists who promoted the human-centered values of ancient Greece and Rome. Humanist ideals were soon influencing the arts, literature, philosophy, science, religion, and politics in Italy. During the early fifteenth century, innovations of the Italian Renaissance began spreading into the rest of Europe and reached a peak in the sixteenth century.) Among them were Christopher Marlowe, Edmund Spenser, and Ben Jonson. Others like Thomas Dekker (1572–1632), George Chapman (1559–1634), Anthony Mundy (c. 1560–1633), and William Shakespeare seemingly did not. It is also important to consider that drama was flourishing in England during the late sixteenth and early seventeenth centuries. Many professional writers were needed to turn out a continuous stream of high-quality plays that satisfied the tastes of audiences. The plays therefore had to be well crafted and profitable. Unlike Oxford and other noblemen, professional writers such as

Shakespeare had a need for financial success, both to express themselves and to make a living. Thus, Shakespeare's supporters argue, this fact should exclude anyone from the noble class as being the true author, since aristocrats would not have devoted their lives to writing for commercial gain.

Joins Lord Chamberlain's Men

Shakespeare arrived in London at a crucial time, when new forms of drama were emerging in England. As the dominant city in the country, London was the center of this new and flourishing drama. In 1576 James Burbage (1531–1597), a former furniture maker, had built a theater at Shoreditch, northeast of the city. It was called the Theatre, perhaps because there were no others. There was plenty of dramatic activity at inn yards, churches, and mansions, but not in permanent theater buildings. Burbage and his colleagues built their theater outside the city to be free of authorities, who tended to be suspicious of theater activity as subversive (anti-government), ungodly, and unhealthy. Richard Burbage (c. 1567–1619), James's son, became Shakespeare's lifelong friend and the leading actor in his major tragedies, such as *Richard III, Hamlet,* and *Othello.* Some of Shakespeare's early plays may have been performed at the Theatre, though it is not known what acting company or companies he may have joined before 1594. That year his name appeared on a list of the Lord Chamberlain's Men, a company that performed chiefly at the Theatre in Shoreditch.

The Theatre appears to have been octagonal (eight-sided) or otherwise many-sided in design, with a seating capacity for perhaps three thousand spectators. More prosperous audience members sat in wooden galleries, while the less well-to-do stood in the "yard" in front of a large rectangular stage. The stage measured about 43 by 27 feet (13 by 8 meters). This platform stood 5 feet (1.5 meters) or so above the floor of the yard. Backstage was a "tiring house" where the actors attired themselves and made their entrances and exits through two or three doors. A gallery above the doors in the tiring house wall may have accommodated well-to-do spectators at times but could also be used for acting scenes. The main stage had a least one trap door in it, and probably supported two pillars

that held up a roof partly covering the stage. The roof could also represent "heavens" from which descents and ascents were made by means of machinery, such as ropes and pulleys. The Theatre was dismantled in 1599 by the Lord Chamberlain's Men after a dispute with the landlord. It was then re-assembled on the south side of the Thames River as the famous Globe Theater. The Globe was recreated in the late twentieth century on a location near the original site.

An illustration of the Globe Theater as it appeared during Shakespeare's time.
Reproduced by permission of The Folger Shakespeare Library.

Achieves innovations in drama

Shakespeare began his professional life in a theater such as that just described. His first known play was probably *The Comedy of Errors* (1590), a comedy (play based on humor) with a complex plot involving two sets of identical twins. This was followed by a romantic comedy, *The Two Gentlemen of Verona* (1591), that tells stories of a faithful girl who educates her fickle lover, a girl dressed as a boy, and happy marriages at the end. *Love's Labour's Lost* (1593), another romantic comedy, deals with the attempt of three young men to withdraw from the world and women for three years to study in their king's "little Academe." The men quickly abandon their plans, however, when a group of young ladies comes to lodge nearby. His first chronicle plays were *Henry VI* (1592) and *Richard III* (1594). These dramas dealt with the tumultuous events of English history between the death of King Henry V in 1422 and the accession of Henry VII in 1485. At the time they marked the most ambitious attempt in English theater to present epic drama (a play that portrays events over a long period of time). Shakespeare's first tragedy, *Titus Andronicus* (1593), reveals similar ambition. Though the modern reader or viewer may think the play is simply a chamber of horrors—the plot is full of mutilations and murders—Shakespeare succeeded in outdoing other English playwrights in the lurid tradition of the revenge play (drama in which the main character seeks revenge on someone who has wronged him). For twenty more years he continued to master and perfect all of these forms—comedy, history, and tragedy—as one of the most productive and brilliant playwrights in history.

Perfects the sonnet

During much of 1593 and 1594 English theaters were closed down because of the plague, a widespread outbreak of disease. Shakespeare therefore turned to writing nondramatic poetry to make a living. Again he excelled in his chosen craft by producing *Venus and Adonis* and the tragic *Rape of Lucrece*. Both poems carry the sophisticated techniques of Elizabethan narrative verse to their highest point, drawing on Renaissance mythological and symbolic traditions. Shakespeare's most famous poems were his 154 sonnets (published in 1609). They are considered the supreme English examples of the sonnet form, which was introduced by the Italian poet **Petrarch** (1304–1374; see entry) at the beginning of the Renaissance and was now in vogue throughout Europe. Shakespeare used the fourteen-line sonnet, with its fixed rhyme scheme, to express emotions and ideas ranging from the frivolous to the tragic. The sonnets are dedicated to "Mr. W. H.," whose identity remains a mystery. Scholars also cannot determine whether there was a real-life "dark lady" or an unfaithful friend, who are the subjects of a number of the poems.

After the theaters reopened in 1594, Shakespeare returned to writing plays because he had been writing poetry only to make money. He became the principal writer for the Lord Chamberlain's Men. In addition to performing as a regular actor, he was a "sharer," or partner, in the group of artist-managers who ran the entire operation. For the Lord Chamberlain's Men, Shakespeare produced a steady outpouring of plays. Among them were the comedies *The Taming of the Shrew* (1594), *A Midsummer Night's Dream* (1595), *The Merchant of Venice* (1596), *Much Ado about Nothing* (1598), and *The Merry Wives of Windsor* (1599). In the year 1600 alone he wrote *As You Like It,* and *Twelfth Night.* Shakespeare's only tragedies of the period are among his most familiar plays: *Romeo and Juliet* (1596), *Julius Caesar* (1599), and *Hamlet* (1601). Continuing his interest in the chronicle, Shakespeare wrote *King John* (1596), *Richard II* (1595), the two-part *Henry IV* (1597), and *Henry V* (1599). At the end of Queen Elizabeth's reign he wrote works that are often called his "problem plays." For example, *All's Well That Ends Well* (1602) is a romantic comedy that presents sexual relations between men and women in a harsh light. The tragicomic (a combination of tragedy and comedy) *Measure for Measure* (1604) suggests that modern urban hopelessness was settling on London.

Writes great tragedies

When King James I (1566–1625; ruled 1603–25) took the throne of England in 1603, he became the patron of the Lord Chamberlain's Men. The name of the company was then changed to the King's Men. During the next five years Shakespeare wrote fewer but perhaps even finer plays: *Othello* (1604), *King Lear* (1605), *Macbeth* (1606), *Antony and Cleopatra* (1607–08), and *Coriolanus* (1607–08). Each in its own way is a drama of alienation (being withdrawn from or outside society), which continues to be relevant to the lives of people in the twenty-first century. These tragedies present an astonishing series of worlds different from one another, in language that exceeds anything Shakespeare had done before. He also created some of his most complex and vivid characters and used a variety of new structural techniques.

A final group of plays took a turn in a new direction. Commonly called the "romances," *Pericles* (1607), *Cymbeline* (1609), *The Winter's Tale* (1611), and *The Tempest* (1611) were tragicomedies, which had been growing popular since the early years of the century. Shakespeare turned this fashionable mode into high art. *The Winter's Tale* is considered one of his best plays, while *The Tempest* is the most popular. After completing *The Tempest,* Shakespeare retired to Stratford. In 1613 he returned to London to compose *Henry VIII* and *The Two Noble Kinsmen.* He died in 1616, at age fifty-two. Shakespeare's work has continued to seem to each generation like its own most precious discovery. His value to his own age is suggested by the fact that, in 1623, two fellow actors gathered his plays together and published them in a form known as the Folio edition. Without their efforts, since Shakespeare was not interested in publication, many of the plays would not have survived.

For More Information

Books

Dommermuth-Costa, Carol. *William Shakespeare*. Minneapolis: Lerner Publications Co., 2002.

Garfield, Leon. *Shakespeare Stories II*. Boston: Houghton Mifflin Co., 1995.

The Oxford Companion to Shakespeare. Michael Dobson and Stanley Wells, editors. Oxford: Oxford University Press, 2001.

The Riverside Shakespeare. G. Blakemore Evans and others, editors. New York: Houghton Mifflin, 1997.

Thrasher, Thomas. *William Shakespeare*. San Diego, Calif.: Lucent Books, 1999.

Web Sites

Shakespeare Resource Center. [Online] Available http://www.bardweb.net/, April 5, 2002.

"Shakespeare, William." *Internet Editions*. [Online] Available http://web.uvic.ca/shakespeare/Annex, April 5, 2002.

"Shakespeare, William." *MSN Encarta*. [Online] Available http://encarta.msn.com/find/Concise.asp?z=1&pg=2&ti=761562101, April 5, 2002.

Süleyman I

1494
1566
Szigetvár, Hungary

Sultan

Süleyman I, who ruled from 1520 until 1566, was the last great sultan, or king, of the Ottoman Empire. The empire was a vast kingdom in the part of Asia called the Near East and in North Africa. The Ottoman Empire was formed in the 1300s, when the Ottoman Turks conquered the Byzantine Empire, the eastern part of the former Roman Empire, which was based in Constantinople (present-day Istanbul, Turkey). The Ottoman Turks were Muslims, or followers of Islam (a religion founded by the prophet Muhammad), from Turkey. Süleyman was named after King Solomon (tenth century B.C.), the king of ancient Israel, whom the *Qur'an* (Koran; the holy book of Islam) describes as the ideal monarch because he had the quality of *'adale,* or justice. In Islamic history Süleyman is known as the second Solomon, and his reign is considered the time of the greatest justice and harmony achieved by any Islamic state. Süleyman actively worked to enlarge the Ottoman Empire while maintaining Islamic principles. He gained a reputation as a firm and just lawgiver and a brilliant military leader.

"Slave of God, master of the world, I am Suleyman and my name is read in all the prayers in all the cities of Islam. I am the Shah of Baghdad and Iraq, Caesar of all the lands of Rome, and the Sultan of Egypt."

Süleyman I quoted in Suleyman the Magnificent. [Online] Available http:// www.wsu.edu: 8001/~dee/ OTTOMAN/SULEYMAN.HTM, April 5, 2002.

Süleyman I. ©Ali Meyer/Corbis. Reproduced by permission of Corbis Corporation.

Known as the "Magnificent"

Süleyman I was the son of Sultan Selim I (the Grim; 1470–1520). Unlike Selim, who neglected European affairs in favor of unifying Ottoman power, Süleyman devoted himself to conducting the *jihad* (Islamic holy war) in Europe. His success in expanding the Ottoman Empire during his reign, mainly through military successes, gained him the nickname of *kanuni* (lawgiver). In Europe he was known as the "Magnificent." Among Süleyman's greatest achievements was making the Ottoman Empire into a mighty sea power. In 1538 the Ottoman navy defeated Andrea Doria (1466–1560), the famous admiral from the Italian city-state of Genoa, in a battle at Preveza, Greece. The Ottomans now had control of the eastern half of the region around the Mediterranean Sea, from Egypt to Algeria. As the protector of Islam, Süleyman also invaded and annexed, or claimed, other Islamic states. For instance, he annexed Arabia, asserting that the ruling families had abandoned the true Islamic faith.

Süleyman ruled at a time when Europeans were mobilizing forces to prevent an Ottoman invasion. For centuries Europeans had feared that they would be overtaken by the Muslims. Not only did Europeans consider Muslims to be pagans (those who have no religion or worship more than one god), but they also thought the inhabitants of Asia and North Africa were racially and culturally inferior to themselves. Nevertheless, the Renaissance was also heavily influenced by Ottoman culture. (The Renaissance was a cultural revolution that began in Italy in the mid-1300s. It was initiated by scholars called humanists who promoted the human-centered values of ancient Greece and Rome.) In fact, European scholars had been visiting cultural centers in the East since the Crusades (1096–1291), holy wars waged by Christians to recapture the Holy Land, or present-day Palestine, from the Muslims. (Palestine is considered holy by Jews, Christians, and Muslims, all of whose religions started there.) Similarly, Muslims viewed Europeans as a threat to Islam. The Ottoman Empire was beginning to shrink as a result of European conquests. Portugal was trying to dominate trade with India and had invaded several Muslim cities in eastern Africa. Russians, considered by Ottomans to be European, were moving into central Asia. Süleyman therefore set out to preserve the principles of Islam by preventing European occupation of Ottoman territory.

Süleyman, "master of all lands"

Süleyman I was the greatest sultan in Islamic history. In various inscriptions (texts written on monuments and buildings) he described himself as the divinely appointed ruler not only of the Ottoman Empire but also of "the lands of Rome" (the Holy Roman Empire):

> Slave of God, powerful with the power of God, deputy of God on earth, obeying the commands of the Qur'an and enforcing them throughout the world, master of all lands, the shadow of God over all nations, Sultan of Sultans in all the lands of Persians and Arabs, the propagator of

[one who implements] Sultanic laws (Nashiru kawanin al-Sultaniyye), the tenth Sultan of the Ottoman Khans, Sultan, son of Sultan, Suleyman Khan.

> Slave of God, master of the world, I am Suleyman and my name is read in all the prayers in all the cities of Islam. I am the Shah of Baghdad and Iraq, Caesar of all the lands of Rome, and the Sultan of Egypt. I seized the Hungarian crown and gave it to the least of my slaves.

Source: Suleyman the Magnificent. [Online] Available http://www.wsu.edu:8001/~dee/ OTTOMAN/SULEYMAN.HTM, April 5, 2002.

Initiates Ottoman strategy in Europe

Süleyman was gaining prominence on the world stage at a time when his European rival, **Charles V** (1500–1558; see entry), was distracted by social and religious upheaval in his own kingdoms. As the Holy Roman Emperor and king of Spain, Charles was a member of the powerful Habsburg family, who controlled central Europe and Spain. He reigned over the largest empire in the Western (non-Asian) history, and he was expanding his territory into the Americas. Nevertheless, he was preoccupied with fighting off challenges to Habsburg power in France and contending with the Protestant Reformation in Germany. (The Reformation had begun as an isolated movement to make changes within the Roman Catholic Church, then escalated into social and political unrest among Protestants and Catholics in the German states.)

Süleyman's understanding of European politics contributed to Ottoman successes. He took advantage of the turmoil in Europe by seeking to destabilize both the Holy Roman Empire and the Roman Catholic Church. He was able to advance his goals through alliances with certain European powers and then playing rival European states against one another. Süleyman moved first in Hungary. This region held little regard for Charles at the moment, so Süleyman knew he could easily win a conflict with the Habsburg rulers of Austria, who also controlled Hungary. In 1521 Süleyman took Belgrade, Serbia. He then defeated the Hungarian king, Louis II (1506–1526; ruled 1516–26), in a decisive battle at Mohács, Hungary, in 1526. He even attacked Vienna, Austria, in 1528.

As Europe was splitting into Catholic and Protestant states, Süleyman became directly involved in European politics. In 1536 he formed an alliance with **Francis I** (1494–1547; see entry), the king of France, against the Habsburgs, a move that had long-range consequences. For the next three centuries the Ottomans pursued the policy of seeking alliances that would keep European states at odds with one another. The immediate impact in the sixteenth century was to keep Charles V off balance. Charles was trying to avoid civil war among Catholics and Protestants in Germany while pursuing Habsburg imperial goals in France. At the same time Charles's brother, Ferdinand I (1503–1564; later Holy Roman emperor 1558–64), needed Protestant financial support while pursuing his claims to the Hungarian throne. The goals of both Charles and Ferdinand, which involved military confrontation with the Turks, were exploited by the Protestant princes of German of states. The princes received funds from Süleyman in their efforts to establish Lutheranism in Germany in 1555. Many historians note that Protestantism would never have succeeded in Europe without Süleyman's support.

Presides over the golden age

Süleyman's reign was known as the golden age of Ottoman culture. The sultan promoted architectural development, commissioning the construction of public baths, bridges, religious schools, and grand mosques (Islamic houses of worship). In 1557 the Turkish architect Sinan (1489–1588) completed the Süleymaniye Mosque in Istanbul. Süleyman also supported other fine arts. At the studio in his palace, twenty-nine artists—half of whom were Europeans—created miniature paintings that represented an innovation in Islamic art.

Süleyman himself made contributions to Islamic culture. He was not only an accomplished goldsmith (one who crafts objects from gold) but a fine poet. The sciences, theology, and the judicial system also flourished under his regime. Süleyman had a reputation as a great lawgiver, mainly because of the military, educational, and legal reforms enacted during his reign. Some historians observe, however, that such a reputation is somewhat exaggerated. Most of the laws were designed to eliminate corruption and to restore the fundamental principles of the *Kanoun Namé,* the basic Ottoman legislation that had been handed down earlier, by Mehmed II the Conqueror (1432–1481; ruled 1444–46, 1451–81). Süleyman's place in history is that of the last sultan who maintained and enlarged the Islamic empire.

The final years of Süleyman's reign were marked by repeated failures and a bitter dispute over who would succeed him to the throne. His favorite wife, Roxelana, began to conspire against his eldest son, Mustafa, in favor of her two sons, Beyazid and Selim. Aware of Roxelana's intentions, Mustafa built up his own faction, or rival group. Süleyman could see that Mustafa was making political moves, so he took it as a sign of an impending mutiny, or rebellion. As a result, Süleyman had Mustafa executed in 1553. When Roxelana died, Beyazid and Selim began to quarrel. Beyazid was victorious over Selim and staged a revolt, but he met defeat and was forced to flee to Persia. The shah, or leader, of Persia was bribed by Selim and Beyazid was returned home, where he was executed. When Süleyman died during the siege of Szigetvár, Hungary, in 1566, Selim succeeded him as Selim II (ruled 1566–74).

During the next century the Ottoman Empire went into decline. One reason was that the role of the sultan had been weakened. For instance, Murad IV (ruled 1623–40) was the last ruler to command his army in battle. Another reason for the decline was that powerful military families protected their own interests, often ignoring the central government, the *Bâbiâli*. In 1571 the Ottoman navy, led by Selim II, was defeated by Holy Roman fleets under the command of the Spanish-born general John of Austria (1545–1578) at Lepanto (now Návpaktos), a seaport in Greece on the strait (thin strip of land) between the Gulfs of Corinth and Patras. As a result of John of Austria's victory, Ottoman control of the Mediterranean had come to an end. Finally, the Safavid ruler 'Abbās I (1571–1629; ruled 1588–1629) conquered Baghdad in Iraq. After concluding a peace treaty with the Safavids in 1639, the Ottomans tried to seize territory in Hungary. For the remainder of the seventeenth century the Ottoman Empire continued to weaken in a power struggle with the Habsburgs of Austria. In 1699 Turkey signed the Treaty of Karlowitz, renouncing Hungary and ending the possibility of Ottoman military conquests in the region.

For More Information

Books

Atil, Esin. *Suleymanname: The Illustrated History of Suleyman the Magnificent.* New York: H. N. Abrams, 1986.

Merriman, Roger Bigelow. *Suleiman the Magnificent.* New York: Cooper Square Publishers, 1966.

Video Recordings

Suleyman the Magnificent. National Gallery of Art and Metropolitan Museum of Art; Home Vision, 1987.

Web Sites

Hooker, Richard. *Suleyman the Magnificent.* [Online] Available http://www.wsu.edu:8001/~dee/OTTOMAN/SULEYMAN.HTM, April 5, 2002.

"Suleyman the I." *Infoplease.com.* [Online] Available http://www.infoplease.com/ce6/people/A0847149.html, April 5, 2002.

Teresa de Ávila

1515
Ávila, Spain
1582
Alba, Spain

Nun, mystic

Teresa de Ávila (also known as Teresa of Jesus) was the founder of the Reformed Discalced (Barefoot) Carmelite Convent of San Jose. She is most famous today for her experiences as a mystic, which she described in her autobiography, *Life* (now titled *The Life of Saint Teresa;* published in1611), and numerous other books.

Teresa was born Teresa de Alhumada in 1515 on a farm near Ávila, Spain. Her father was Alonso (Pina) de Cepeda, son of a wealthy Jewish businessman who had converted to Christianity, and her mother was Beatriz de Ahumada, a farmer's daughter. Teresa's Jewish grandfather had become a Christian because unconverted Jews were not allowed to live in Spain. In 1474 the Spanish monarchs, or rulers, King Ferdinand II (1452–1516) of Aragon and Queen Isabella (1451–1504) of Castile started a church court called the Spanish Inquisition to enforce Christianity as the sole religion of Spain. Their adviser was Tomás de Torquemada (pronounced tor-kay-MAH-thah; 1420–1498), a Dominican monk (member of a religious order founded by Saint Dominic). In 1487 Torquemada was promoted to grand inquisitor (supreme head of the

Teresa de Ávila.

353

court), and he set out to rid Spain of Jews called Marranos (also Conversos) who had supposedly converted to Christianity but did not actually practice the religion. Those who did not confess their sins or undergo genuine conversion were severely punished or executed. Practicing Jews were segregated and forced to wear an identifying badge.

Enters convent

When Teresa was fourteen, her mother died in childbirth, leaving behind ten children. In her autobiography, Teresa recalled that when she was sixteen she would sneak out of the house to meet with a man she loved. She said her downfall was a "love for good conversation." After gossip about the relationship reached her father, he took her to Our Lady of Grace, a cloistered convent nearby. A cloistered convent is a religious house for women that is enclosed within walls. Women who live in a convent are called nuns, and they devote their lives entirely to the church. Cloistered nuns are not permitted to go outside the walls of the convent. Some convents are not cloistered, and the nuns are free to have contact with the outside world.

Teresa stayed at Our Lady of Grace until 1532, when she became ill with a weak heart. She also suffered from rheumatoid arthritis (painful inflammation and swelling of the joints) for the rest of her life. After recuperating for nearly three years at her sister's farmhouse, Teresa decided to become a nun. One of her greatest fears was going to hell (the place it is commonly believed sinners go after death) when she died, and she claimed that she wanted to be a nun because of that fear. She told her father about her decision, but he was determined not to give her to the church. Teresa then ran away to the Carmelite Convent of the Encarnacion (Incarnation), where she became a nun in 1537 and took the name of Teresa de Jesus. The convent, which was uncloistered, offered great freedom to Carmelites. They wore perfume, jewelry, and colorful sashes. Later, Teresa called it "an inn just off the road of hell." While she was there, she met a nobleman and fell in love, an experience that was disturbing for her.

About a year later, she became ill again and left the Carmelites to recuperate at her sister's house. Doctors said she was fatally ill with consumption (a disease of the lungs that causes the wasting away of the body). One of her uncles had given her religious books to read the last time she was ill. This time, he had discovered "mystical theology" (a religious philosophy based on intense spiritual experiences) and gave her a copy of *The Third Spiritual Alphabet* by Francisco de Osuna, a Franciscan monk (member of the order of Saint Francis). Teresa began collecting books on the new theology and entered the mystical stage of her life. When she became strong enough, she decided to go to a healer for a "cure." She became so ill during her trip, however, that her father took her home to die. For four days Teresa lay in a coma, or state of unconsciousness, so severe she was thought to be dead. She slowly recovered, however, and insisted on going back to the Carmelite convent, where she spent the next three years in the infirmary (hospital at the convent) with a paralyzed leg. After her recovery, she rejoined the Carmelites and spent the next three years living from day to day with no sense of purpose and pursuing frivolous pleasures.

Experiences conversion, leaves convent

In 1543, Teresa's father died and she went through a long struggle with inner conflict. Although she suffered internally over the next ten years, the people around her saw her as a "distinguished lady" who was "gay and witty." Teresa agonized over her feelings for men, especially a nobleman and priest named Garcia de Toledo. In 1554 she experienced a conversion, or spiritual change, when she saw a statue of the wounded Christ (Jesus of Nazareth, founder of Christianity). Then someone gave her a copy of *Confessions* by Saint Augustine (354–430), an early church leader. She identified with the spiritual suffering described by Augustine and realized that she was not damned (destined for hell, or eternal suffering). As a result, she turned her attention to important issues that threatened the church. In 1556 Teresa asked for permission to leave the convent. The Carmelites allowed her to leave, since her practices in penance (seeking forgiveness of sin) and prayer were considered extreme compared to the casual lifestyle at the convent.

For the next three years Teresa lived with a friend, Dona Guiomar de Ulloa (Yomar). With the help of Juan de

John of the Cross

John of the Cross (1542–1591) was one of the most important mystical writers in the Catholic tradition. Along with Teresa de Ávila, he played a leading role in the reform of the Carmelites.

John of the Cross was born Juan de Yepes at Fontiveros, Spain. In 1563 he became a novice at the monastery of Saint Ana in Medina. His superiors sent him to the University of Salamanca, where he was ordained a priest in 1567. The following year Teresa visited the Medina monastery to discuss the possibility of including male monasteries in her Reformed Discalced Carmelite order. Both John and the prior (head of a monastery) of the house joined Teresa's order, and John was the first friar (member of a religious order) accepted into the new monastery, Duruelo. John joined Teresa as confessor in the unreformed Carmelite convent of Ávila, of which she had become prioress.

Meanwhile, the opposition between Reformed Discalced Carmelites and Calced Carmelites, which had existed from the beginning, took on alarming proportions. In 1575 John was abducted and imprisoned by the Calced friars. He was set free at the request of the papal nuncio (pope's representative in the government). But he was imprisoned again in 1577, and this time he had to escape. For safety he stayed in remote places in Andalusia (a region in southern Spain). During those years of obscurity he wrote most of his mystical works. After the two branches of the Carmelites were finally split, John remained in the south but regained status as vicar provincial (deputy district head of a religious order). In 1588 he returned to Castile as prior of the house of Segovia and as councilor, or adviser, of the provincial (province). Because of his disagreement with the radical, innovative provincial, he was soon removed from office and sent back to Andalusia. He died after an excruciating agony in 1591. John of the Cross was declared a saint in 1726 and pronounced a doctor of the church in 1926. (A doctor of the church is one who defends Roman Catholic teachings.) The Saint John's works consist of poetry and mystical commentaries that he wrote on some of his poems. Best known are *The Spiritual Canticle, The Living Flame of Love, The Dark Night of the Soul,* and *Ascent of Mount Carmel.*

to Alba and even though she was ill, she went willingly. After arriving in Alba, she went to the convent, where she suffered a hemorrhage (uncontrolled bleeding) and was taken to the infirmary. Teresa knew she was dying, but she was joyful at the end. Witnesses said that a sweet fragrance filled the room at the time of her death. Teresa was buried at the convent chapel in Alba, although many friends protested that she should be buried in Ávila. Her tomb emitted the mysterious sweet fragrance and miracles were reported.

Nine months later, Gracian, a Reformed Carmelite superior, had Teresa's body exhumed, or removed from the grave. Although her robes were rotting, her body was well preserved. Gracian cut off her left hand, then reburied her in the tomb. He took the hand back to Ávila where he cut off one finger to use as a talisman, or good luck charm. Three years later, Gracian convinced the Chapter of the Discalced to exhume her body and take it to Ávila. They agreed to leave one arm in Alba to console the nuns there. Teresa's body was still preserved. The Discalceds considered this a supernatural occurrence since she had not been embalmed (preserved with special fluids after death). The duchess was outraged and the duke convinced the pope to order Teresa's body to be returned to Alba. By the eighteenth century, her body had been exhumed many times for examination and little by little body parts, bones, and pieces of flesh were missing. When Teresa's heart was removed, it appeared to have a knife wound that was burned around the edges. Teresa was canonized, declared a saint, in 1622, and in 1970 she was the first woman to be named a doctor of the church."

For More Information

Books

Medwick, Cathleen. *Teresa of Avila: the Progress of a Soul*. New York: Alfred A. Knopf, 1999.

Teresa de Ávila. *The Life of Saint Teresa*. J. M. Cohen, translator. New York: Penguin Books, 1957.

Web Sites

Knight, Kevin. "Teresa of Ávila." *Catholic Encyclopedia*. [Online] Available http://www.newadvent.org/cathen/14515b.htm, April 5, 2002.

Teresa of Ávila. [Online] Available http://www.karmel.at/eng/teresa.htm, April 5, 2002.

"Teresa de Ávila." *Way of Perfection*. [Online] Available http://www.ccel.org/t/teresa/way/main.html, April 5, 2002.

Gustav I Vasa

**May 12, c. 1496
Uppland, Sweden
1560
Stockholm, Sweden**

King, rebel

Gustav I Vasa. *Reproduced by permission of Archive Photos, Inc.*

Gustav I Vasa is considered the founder of the modern Swedish nation. During the Protestant Reformation he adopted Lutheranism as the state religion. He was also the first European ruler to form a national citizens' army, and he developed the Swedish navy into a major maritime (sea) power. Abandoning the tradition of electing a king, he established a hereditary monarchy that resulted in a Vasa dynasty (line of rulers from the same family). During his thirty-seven-year reign, Gustav I consolidated Sweden's independence and laid the foundation for the country's greatness in the next century.

Fights bravely in battle

Gustav was born in Uppland, Sweden, around 1496. He was the eldest son of Erik Johansson Vasa, lord of Rydboholm, who was a knight (nobleman soldier) and councilor of state. Information is lacking about Gustav's childhood and youth. He took the throne at age twenty-seven, during a tumultuous period in Swedish history. The crisis dated back to 1397, when Sweden, Denmark, and Norway were politically united by the Union of Kalmar. Under this arrangement the aristocracies (nobility, or upper class) of these countries, which shared similar cultures and languages, agreed to elect their kings. They took this step to fight off the efforts of German princes to gain influence over them. The Union frequently broke down throughout the fifteenth century, however, and it came to an end in the early sixteenth century as a result of conflict between the Danish king Christian II (1481–1559; ruled Sweden 1520–23) and the Swedish popular leader Sten Sture (called the Younger; c. 1492–1520).

Sten Sture took the title of regent of Sweden and was virtually an independent monarch, or ruler, but he still ruled on behalf of Christian II of Denmark. Like most Renaissance princes, Christian was eager to strengthen his power. He isolated Sten Sture diplomatically and then attacked Sweden directly in 1517. His pretext was that he had come to rescue Gustav Trolle (1488–1535), the archbishop of Uppsala in Sweden, who believed Sten Sture was trying to diminish the rights and privileges of the Roman Catholic Church. Seeing Trolle as a threat, Sten Sture won the assent of the *Riksdag,* or Swedish Estates (a gathering of the principal nobility), to demolish the archbishop's fortress at Almare-Staket. Sten Sture met and defeated Christian II on the battlefield of Brännkyrka in 1518. Among Sten Sture's troops was the twenty-two-year-old Gustav Vasa, who fought courageously.

In the treaty that followed this conflict, the victorious Sten Sture handed over young Gustav to the Danish king as a pledge of his good intentions. Christian II took Gustav back to a mild form of captivity in Denmark. When Gustav heard news of renewed fighting between Denmark and Sweden, he escaped and made his way to Lübeck, Germany. Lübeck was one of the cities in the powerful trade network, the Hanseatic League, which dominated trade in the Baltic Sea, northern Germany, and Scandinavia (see accompanying box). In 1520 Christian convinced Pope Leo X (1475–1521; reigned 1513–21) to excommunicate (expel from the church) Sten Sture and members of the Swedish Estates for their insulting behavior toward Archbishop Trolle. Christian renewed his attack, this time defeating Swedish forces at the Battle of Lake Asunden. Sten Sture was killed in the fighting. Christian then seized Stockholm, the capital of Sweden. On November 8, 1520, he presided over the "Bloodbath of Stockholm," in which his Danish soldiers chopped off the heads of nearly one hundred prominent Swedes who had supported Sten Sture. The massacre continued in the Swedish provinces in the weeks that followed.

Elected King Gustav I Vasa

The surviving Swedes cast about frantically for a leader and found one in Gustav Vasa. With help from supporters in Lübeck he had made his way home and discovered that his father, his brother-in-law, and two of his uncles had been killed in the Bloodbath of Stockholm. Gustav, therefore, had a powerful motive for taking up the fight against the Danes. He began to gather followers, and won his first victory over Christian at Västerås in the spring of 1521. Advancing on Stockholm, Gustav met the surviving Swedish aristocrats who appointed him regent (one who governs in the place of an official ruler). At first the aristocrats thought they could use Gustav to their advantage, but they gradually recognized his skills as a genuine leader and his determination not to be manipulated. In 1523 Gustav took control of Sweden with the backing of Lübeck merchants, who sent him mercenary, or hired, soldiers and ships to blockade (a method of preventing shipping into and out of an area) the remaining Danish military posts. In exchange for aid from Lübeck, Gustav had to promise major trading concessions. The Swedish aristocracy then elected him King Gustav I at Strängnäs.

The most immediate threat to Gustav's reign came not from Christian II of Denmark but from the supporters of Sten Sture. Among them was Sten Sture's widow Christina Gyllenstierna and young son Nils. They planned to make Nils king and were angry that Gustav had appointed some of Sten Sture's old enemies to major state offices. They rebelled in 1524. Claiming to be true Swedish patriots, they recruited hungry peasants who had admired Sten Sture's patriotism and were now suffering from poor harvests and high taxes. The determined Gustav defeated the rebels at their stronghold, the castle of Kalmar, in 1525.

For the first years of his reign, Gustav was beholden to the city of Lübeck. Lübeck merchants managed to dislodge Christian II from the Danish throne and install their own

The Hanseatic League

The Hanseatic League was a trading network formed by German towns after 1100. A major reason for the league's development was the lack of a powerful national government that could support extensive commerce and provide safe passage for merchants when they traveled to foreign lands. As a result, companies of merchants made agreements that guaranteed mutual protection, exclusive trading rights, and trade monopolies (domination without competition) whenever possible. Implementing these agreements, the merchants began building towns that were closer together.

At first the league was controlled by a dozen or so German towns, known as Hansa, in the Baltic and Rhineland regions.

Originally "hansa" referred to an association of warriors, but the term soon denoted a tax imposed on foreign merchants. Gradually, the word came to mean a group of merchants in a particular city who were engaged in trade with foreign lands. Finally the German "Hansa" signified a vast community of urban merchants who did business in the Baltic Sea and the North Sea. Three stages marked the expansion of the Hanseatic League: It was initiated during the period 1100 to 1200; it reached its height in the years 1200 to 1350; and its influence gradually decreased during the two centuries from 1350 to 1550. After 1550 the commercial unity of the Hansa fell apart, although certain cities such as Lübeck, Bremen, and Hamburg continued to prosper far into the modern period.

king, Frederick I (1471–1553; ruled 1524–53). Sweden and Denmark now owed debts to Lübeck and both feared Christian II's vengeance. He was related to the most powerful man in Europe, Holy Roman Emperor **Charles V** (1500–1558; see entry). Together Swedes, Danes, and Lübeckers evicted one of Christian's generals from the strategic island of Gotland in 1526. In the years that followed, the new kings of Denmark and Sweden found other common points of interest, despite remaining tensions from the war that had broken the Union of Kalmar. The unsentimental Gustav never let gratitude toward Lübeck get the better of him. Gustav felt no obligation to Lübeck and he set out to diversify Sweden's trade rather than see it funneled into Lübeck on disadvantageous terms. Thus he began trade negotiations with Holland and signed a trading agreement with Prussia in 1526.

Dismantles Catholic Church

For Gustav, as for many other rulers seeking to enlarge their power, the Protestant Reformation (a movement to reform the Roman Catholic Church) was an irresistible temptation. Like every other part of Europe, Sweden had long been subject to intervention and taxation from the pope. A monarch, therefore, could benefit from gaining control over church affairs and properties. Gustav was not a rich man, and he had pressing debts from the recent war of independence, which he could not pay from the small revenues of his estates. (At that time monarchs funded wars themselves.) The church, by contrast, received from tithes (one-tenth of the income of all Catholics) alone almost five times as much as the king's annual income. It also owned estates, castles, and other forms of wealth in abundance. Gustav was determined to lay his hands on this wealth.

Gustav realized he could gain control over the church by supporting Protestant reform, which had been initiated by the German priest **Martin Luther** (1483–1546; see entry). In 1517 Luther had presented his Ninety-five Theses, a list of grievances against the church, at Wittenberg, Germany. In the 1520s the reform movement was still called Lutheranism, and a full-fledged Protestant Reformation came about later. Gustav's chancellor (secretary of state), Lars Andreae, had already converted to Lutheranism under the influence of the clergyman Olaus Petri (1493–1552). Petri had been a student in Wittenberg when Luther began his confrontation with the church. Within a year of taking the throne, Gustav was defending the small circle of Lutherans in Stockholm, and he gave his approval to Petri's marriage. (According to Catholic Church law, priests are not permitted to marry.) Most Swedes opposed the changes brought about by the Reformation. The Catholic bishop, Hans Brask of Linköping, tried to coordinate church opposition and stamp out Lutheranism. He warned aristocrats that the king would withdraw their privileges next if they did not resist his designs on the church. Brask could not prevail against the Gustav's counteroffer to his nobles that they could share in any wealth seized from the church. In 1527 the Swedish Estates met in Västerås to decide religious policy. The artful King burst into tears and threatened to abdicate (step down from the thrown) if his plan to strip the churches of their wealth was not endorsed. A new rebel-

lion against the king, led by an imposter pretending to be Sten Sture's son, made the aristocracy afraid of the chaos that might follow. Ignoring Brask's pleas, they agreed to Gustav's plan in the "Recess of Västerås." Although the Recess denied that Sweden was turning to Lutheranism, the actual result was to hasten the dismantling of Swedish Catholicism. Laurentius Petri (1499–1573), brother of Olaus, was appointed the first Lutheran archbishop of Uppsala. In 1541, under his

Gustav I Vasa threatening to abdicate his throne if his plan to strip the churches of their wealth was not endorsed. *©Bettmann/Corbis. Reproduced by permission of Corbis Corporation.*

guidance, a Swedish language Bible marked the most ambitious publishing venture in Swedish history to that date.

The Reformation in Sweden, as in England, left the cathedrals, bishops, and clergy largely undisturbed while monasteries (religious houses for men) and convents (religious houses for women) were gradually eliminated. There was surprisingly little Catholic resistance outside a small circle of theologians, yet the reform process was anything but painless for the clergy. Even those willing to renounce Catholicism and take up Lutheranism witnessed Gustav's plundering of their churches for gold and silver items, candlesticks, and other wealth that could be converted into cash. For himself and his nobles the king seized estates, castles, and lands that had been church property for centuries. This policy led to an uprising of Catholic nobles and peasants in the southwestern provinces of Sweden in 1529, but Gustav soon outwitted the rebels and executed the ringleaders.

In 1531 a more serious threat to Gustav's power came from Christian II, the former king of Denmark. After eight years of exile in Holland, Christian II finally mounted a campaign to regain what he saw as his rightful rule of Sweden and Denmark. Aided by Emperor Charles V, Christian II landed in Norway and advanced quickly at first. He ran out of energy when he met fierce Swedish resistance. Frederick I of Denmark was finally able to capture Christian II in 1532. Christian was imprisoned and confined until his death twenty-six years later.

Wins decisive Count's War

Christian II was more easily disposed of than the Lübeck merchants. Gustav had repeatedly put off repayment of his debts and was eager to bring an end to Lübeck's trading monopoly. In 1534, after a period of complex diplomacy, Lübeck declared war on both Denmark and Sweden for breaking their promises. All of Gustav's enemies who had been driven into exile during the previous decade—including the Sten Sture faction, disaffected Catholics, and his own brother-in-law, John of Hoya—joined forces with Lübeck against him. Swedish historians call this the "Count's War." Gustav responded by again allying with

Frederick I and taking to the battlefield, where he defeated the Lübeckers at the Battle of Halsingborg. From the start of his reign he had been collecting ships, hoping to challenge the trading power of the Hanseatic ports. Now his newly formed navy won victories at Bornholm and the Little Belt in 1535, inaugurating the growth of Swedish naval and maritime power.

Gustav then became obsessed with gathering financial surpluses to safeguard his kingdom. He repeatedly warned his subjects that without military and financial preparedness, events like the Bloodbath of Stockholm could occur again. In the late 1530s he began developing Sweden's one silver mine at Sala. As a royal monopoly it filled Gustav's treasury and cushioned the country against accelerating inflation (price increases). The king also established an iron industry in Sweden and tried to establish direct trade links with Holland and England. The trading ventures did not work out because Swedes had no real experience in trade.

In running his kingdom, Gustav, like most of other European monarchs, tried to free himself from dependence on the aristocracy. According to tradition, government positions were passed from father to son, not on the basis of merit but on the right of inheritance. Gustav wanted to change this system and appoint government officials whose advancement depended on his favor rather than their social position. But recruiting competent civil servants was no easy matter. Most of the aristocrats were hard-drinking and uneducated, with no administrative skills. Sweden's one university, at Uppsala, had fallen into disuse in the second decade of the century. Even though Gustav had become rich, he showed no interest in investing any of his wealth in education. Swedes who wanted an education had to go abroad, while government workers had to be brought in from other countries. This brought problems of a different kind. The most famous example was an era called the "Rule of Secretaries," when two Germans, Georg Norman and Konrad von Pyhy, ran the king's affairs. Neither man knew Swedish history and tradition. They gained the furious resentment of the aristocracy through their tactless methods of running the kingdom and raising revenue. Norman and Pyhy contributed to the worst domestic upheaval of Gustav's entire reign.

Peasants rebel against policies

The Rule of Secretaries, the Reformation, heavy taxation, and the king's autocratic policies contributed to a rebellion in 1542. It was led by Nils Dacke, a prosperous peasant in the Småland district of southern Sweden. Dacke's peasant volunteers outwitted Gustav's German mercenaries for more than a year. Despite early setbacks, the resourceful king was able to isolate Småland with a blockade and an embargo, or prohibition, on trade. He then defeated Dacke at the Battle of Hogsby. To ratify his victory, Gustav convened the Swedish Estates at Västerås in 1544. He persuaded the Estates to convert his elective monarchy into a hereditary one by claiming that without a secure center the nation might again fall victim to a new bloodbath. Such an event would occur, he warned, if foreign powers took advantage of internal turmoil, as they had tried to do with Dacke. In the early years of his reign Gustav had frequently summoned the Estates as a way of assuring broad support for his actions. They had not met since 1529, however, as Gustav had acquired increasing power. For instance, in 1539, without consultation, he had declared that the church was a department of state, making it completely subordinate to the government. Now Gustav wanted the Estates' approval to strengthen his authority once again. He was also trying to rid himself of dependence on mercenary soldiers, who were expensive and unreliable. In their place he wanted to create the nucleus of a citizen-army. Gustav succeeded in both objects, establishing a Vasa dynasty and making Sweden the first country in Europe to have a permanent army of its own farmer-soldiers.

From that time until his death in 1560, Gustav's throne rested secure. In 1554 he even tried to expand his eastern frontier with Russia by going through Finland, which was then a Swedish province. His actions provoked an inconclusive three-year war with Russian Czar Ivan IV (1530–1584; ruled 1533–84). In the meantime, Gustav continued draining church resources and extracting ever-larger sums of money from cities with threats of looming danger. During his lifetime Gustav had three wives. In 1531 he married Katarina of Saxe-Lauenburg. According to an unconfirmed rumor, he killed her with a hammer. He then married Margareta Leijonhufvud in1536 and Katarina Stenbock in1552. Gustav was an irritable and vengeful old man when he died. His reign continued with

Vasa Dynasty Strengthens Sweden

In 1544 Gustav I persuaded the Swedish Estates to abolish the elective monarchy and substitute it with a hereditary one. Thus he took the first step in establishing a Vasa dynasty. He also convinced the Estates to discontinue the practice of using mercenary soldiers to fight wars. In their place Gustav created the nucleus of a citizens' army. Sweden became the first country in Europe to have a permanent army of its own farmer-soldiers.

Gustav I's decisions ultimately led to the strengthening of the Swedish nation. His descendent, Gustav II Adolf (1594–1632; ruled 1611–32), was one of the great Swedish kings. Gustav II's reign brought higher standards of government, such as better administration and tax collection, as well as the rule of law and educational advancement. In 1600, Sweden did not have a central government. By 1626 it boasted the most efficient and well-ordered government in Europe. Gustav II was also one of the world's leading military geniuses. He is credited with creating the first modern army. During his reign he defeated Poland and conquered Livonia. By winning a war with Russia he also acquired Ingermanland and Karelia. In 1620 Sweden entered the Thirty Years' War (1618–48), a political and religious conflict involving major European powers, to join France against the Holy Roman Empire and the Catholic Habsburgs.

At this time Sweden was the foremost Protestant power on the European continent. Although Gustav II Adolf was killed at the Battle of Lützen in 1632, his policies were carried on during the reign of his daughter Christina (1626–1689; ruled 1632–54). She was assisted by his prime minister Axel Oxenstierna (1583–1654).

Under the terms of the Peace of Westphalia (1648), which ended the Thirty Years' War, Sweden acquired a large part of Pomerania, the island of Rügen, Wismar, the sees (church headquarters) of Bremen and Verden, and other German territory. This entitled the Swedish sovereign to three votes in the diet (meeting of church officials and representatives of states in the Holy Roman Empire) of the Holy Roman Empire. Sweden then became the greatest power in the Baltic region. In 1654 Queen Christina abdicated, naming her cousin Charles X Gustav (1622–1660; ruled 1654–60) as her successor. She lived the rest of her life in Rome, Italy. Charles declared war on Poland, initiating the conflict known as the First Northern War (1655–60). Sweden was victorious and, in 1660, under the terms of a treaty called the Peace of Oliva, Poland formally gave the province of Livonia to Sweden. Charles invaded Denmark twice in 1658, gaining provinces in southern Sweden that Denmark had acquired in the sixteenth century.

his son, who took the name Erik XIV (1533–1577; ruled 1560–68) and carried on the expansion of Swedish power. By the 1620s, Sweden was a major player in European politics.

For More Information

Web Sites

"Gustav I Vasa." *Britannica.com*. [Online] Available http://www.britannica.com/eb/article?eu=39368&tocid=0&query=gustaf%20i%20vasa, April 5, 2002.

"Gustavus I." *Learning Network*. [Online] Available http://www.factmonster.com/ce6/people/A0822195.html, April 5, 2002.

Andreas Vesalius

December 31, 1514
Brussels, Belgium
October 15, 1564
Zenta, Greece

Anatomist

Andreas Vesalius was the founder of modern anatomy (the study of the structure of the body). His scientific work and experimental findings revolutionized the study of the human body. Vesalius is remembered principally for his master work, *De humani corporis fabrica*, (On the fabric of the human body) which was published in 1543. However, his primary contribution was the use of more adequate data sampling than that used by his predecessors. Vesalius's work led to more systematic findings and expert demonstrations.

Shows early talent

Andreas Vesalius was born on December 31, 1514, in Brussels, the son of Andries van Wesele and his wife, Isabel Crabbe. Vesalius's paternal ancestors, moved from the German town of Wesel to Brussels in the early fifteenth century and became prominent as physicians and pharmacists. His father served as pharmacist to Margaret of Austria (1480–1530) and later to Holy Roman Emperor **Charles V** (1500–1558; see entry). His great-grandfather, Johannes Wesalia, was the head

Andreas Vesalius.
Photograph courtesy of
The Library of Congress.

of the medical school at the University of Louvain, where Vesalius started his medical studies in 1530. He enrolled at the university under the name Andres van Wesel de Bruxella.

In 1533 Vesalius transferred to the medical school of the University of Paris. One of his two teachers was Johann Guenther von Andernach, a personable man but a poor anatomist. The other was Jacobus Sylvius, who departed from tradition by giving some role to dissection (cutting a bodies apart) in anatomical instructions. Both teachers gave testimony of their student's anatomical expertise. Guenther published a work in 1536 that glowingly recorded Vesalius's discovery of the spermatic vessels. Sylvius, on the other hand, violently disagreed with Vesalius's daring claim that Galen, the great authority in physiology since classical times, wrote on the inner organs of the body without ever seeing them.

Due to the outbreak of war between France and Spain (a conflict called the Italian Wars; 1494–1559), Vesalius had to leave Paris in 1536. Spain was part of the Holy Roman Empire. The empire was headed by Emperor Charles V, who was also king Charles I of Spain. The Holy Roman Empire covered most of central Europe and parts of northern Europe, including the Low Countries. France was not in the Holy Roman Empire, so citizens of the empire living in France when war broke out were required to return to their home countries. As a citizen of the Low Countries, Vesalius therefore had to go back to Louvain, Belgium. On the recommendation of Guenther, Vesalius was permitted to conduct public dissections while he was still a student. He also published *Paraphrase of the Ninth Book of Rhazes*. Rhazes, also known as al-Rasi, was a tenth-century Muslim physician. In this work Vesalius made a considerable effort to substitute Latin terms for the still heavily Arabic medical terminology.

Publishes revolutionary works

Vesalius soon became embroiled in disputes with faculty members, showing both his genius and his quarrelsome nature. He was practically compelled to go the next year to the University of Padua, located in Italy. In December 1537 Vesalius passed his doctoral examination with high honors, and was immediately appointed professor of surgery and

Six anatomical tables

Andreas Vesalius acquired a reputation as a teacher who not only lectured expertly on anatomy, but also performed his own dissections. In 1538, together with his countryman Jan Stephanus van Calcar (1499–c. 1545), Vesalius produced six large charts to illustrate his lectures. Titled *Tabulae anatomicae sex,* (Six anatomical tables), they were based mainly on Galenic precepts. Galen (A.D. 129–c. 199) was a Greek anatomist who lived and worked in Rome. He dissected only animals, not humans. His doctrines, which had become authoritative in many European medical schools during the first half of the sixteenth century, are not correct when applied to human anatomy. Some of Galen's errors, such as a five-lobed liver and an ovine vascular structure in the brain, appeared in Vesalius's six anatomical tables. Vesalius's contemporaries therefore concluded that he still accepted Galen's theories. Several years later, after performing other dissections and acquiring more clinical material, Vesalius denounced Galen's doctrines. A diligent German student, observing these dissections at the University of Bologna, had taken detailed notes recording this dramatic development. The notes went undiscovered until the mid-twentieth century.

anatomy. In his new post he was required to do dissections, and he performed his first dissection in this post in December 1537. His findings led him to write his first work, which appeared in 1538. The publication was six sheets of his anatomical drawings under the title *Tabulae anatomicae sex* (Six anatomical tables; see box). The publication was an instant success, but because of the great demand the sheets soon were reprinted, without Vesalius's authorization, in Cologne, Paris, Strasbourg, and elsewhere. In 1539 he published his essay on bloodletting (a popular cure that involved draining blood from the body), in which he first described the veins that draw blood from the side of the torso (chest and stomach). This opened the way to the study of veins and led ultimately to the discovery of the circulation of blood by the English physician William Harvey (1578–1657).

In 1540 Vesalius began working on an illustrated anatomical text, *De humani corporis fabrica libri septem* (Seven books on the construction of the human body), known as *Fabrica*. While Venice was a center for the new art of printing, Vesalius chose to entrust the printing of this work to the humanist and publisher Johannes Oporinus in Basel, Switzerland. As a result, the woodblocks—blocks of wood on which images are carved for printing illustrations called woodcuts—produced in Venice were loaded on mules and carried over the Alps (a mountain range between France and Switzerland) to Basel. Vesalius then joined Oporinus in Basel. *Fabrica* is one of Vesalius's greatest works, though some parts were better than others. Book one, on the bones, was generally correct but represented no major advance. Book two, on the muscles, was considered a masterpiece, yet book three on blood vessels was not well received. Book four, which concerned the nerves, was a great advance, but it was largely outdated a century later. His treatment of the abdominal organs in book five was considered excellent. Book six dealt with the chest and neck, while book seven was devoted to the brain. Some of the woodcut illustrations in *Fabrica* are among the best of sixteenth-century drawings and probably were executed by Calcar. Vesalius's own drawings were of only moderate value.

Supports experimentation in *Fabrica*

To understand the importance of Vesalius's accomplishments, one must review the contents of *Fabrica*. Its format was among the largest available (slightly larger than a modern newspaper) and runs more than 650 pages, some with quite small type. The title page shows a dramatic representation of a sixteenth-century anatomical dissection. Several pages later, the only authentic portrait of Vesalius appears. Detailed descriptive texts accompany the illustrations, and references in the margins lead readers from one subject to another. The most striking feature of the work is the illustrations, best exemplified by the fourteen plates depicting the progressive dissection of a muscle. Such an integration of the whole human structure had never been accomplished and was not attempted again until late in the seventeenth century, or even well into the eighteenth century.

The scientific principles put forth in the *Fabrica* made an even more lasting impact on Renaissance science than the major advance in knowledge of the body's structure. Vesalius continually reaffirmed his belief that Galen's anatomy was unreliable. He stressed that Galen's work was grounded in the study of animals and therefore could have no direct application to human anatomy. The only reliable authority was independent investigation of human structure. Moreover, because human structures tend to vary, one must study the same structure in a number of bodies before reaching a conclusion. Thus, Vesalius believed in the idea that an experiment must be made many times before it can be verified, a fundamental part of modern science.

While in Basel, Vesalius was asked to dissect the body of an executed criminal, the skeletal remains of which have been placed in the Basel anatomical museum. The printed account was published in 1543. Virtually simultaneously, Vesalius produced a briefer work, titled *Epitome* for use by medical students and those with limited or no anatomical knowledge In *Epitome* the illustrations are more important than the text. The book is arranged for the reader whom Vesalius described as wholly unskilled in dissection. An extremely popular work, *Epitome* was translated into German immediately; *Fabrica,* in contrast, was translated into modern languages only in the twentieth century.

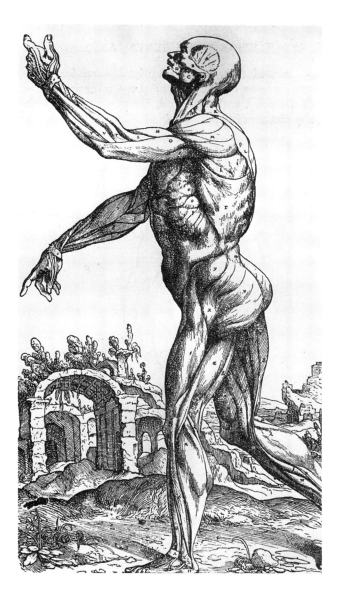

A plate from Vesalius's book *Fabrica* showing the muscles of the human body.
Reproduced by permission of Hulton Archive.

Appointed physician at emperor's court

Vesalius can be compared with other geniuses of his age, such as the Polish astronomer **Nicolaus Copernicus** (1473–1543; see entry), who formulated the theory of the Sun-centered universe, and the English humanist **Thomas More** (1478–1535; see entry), who described a perfect society in *Utopia.* Like Copernicus and More, Vesalius was a daring innovator and a strong traditionalist at the same time. Thus Vesalius, the meticulous observer, did not part with Galen as far as theory was concerned. He was also aware of political realities of his time. No sooner was *Fabrica* published than, at age twenty-nine, Vesalius returned to Padua and sought employment as a physician in the court of Charles V. He was immediately accepted. Vesalius was kept busy treating the emperor, who had a long history of medical ailments. Yet he always visited medical schools while accompanying Charles on his travels throughout the empire. Occasionally, Vesalius was invited to participate in dissections. Consequently, during his employment in imperial service he developed several new techniques in surgery and continued to compile corrections for *Fabrica*.

In 1544 Vesalius married Anne von Hamme and also increased his holdings by a substantial inheritance from his father. In 1546 he published his *Letter on the Chinese Root*, which discussed the merits of the Chinese root, a worthless but very popular medicine. The letter's true significance came from the fact that Vesalius used it to reply to the detractors of his *Fabrica* as well as to amend incorrect statements in the work. In 1553 Vesalius set up private practice as a physician in Brussels, and in 1556 his official ties with the court of Charles V came to an end.

In 1555, thirteen years after *Fabrica*'s initial publication, Vesalius published a second edition, which contains additions and corrections on almost every page. He also expanded on some of the passages because he had become better informed on the details due to his long career and studies. Just as he was about to publish this volume, Charles V abdicated (stepped down from the thrown) the imperial throne and divided his empire between his brother Ferdinand I (1503–1564; ruled 1558–64) and his son, **Philip II** (1527–1598; see entry), who became king of Spain and the Netherlands. Vesalius chose to join Philip's court in Spain as an imperial physician. However, the cultural climate there did not allow for Vesalius's scientific development.

In 1564 Vesalius made a trip to the Holy Land (present-day Israel; a region considered sacred to Jews, Christians, and Muslims). Christians make pilgrimages (religious journeys) to Jerusalem, the town in Israel where Jesus Christ, the founder of Christianity, lived and spread his teachings. Historians have questioned whether Vesalius used the trip as a way to leave Spain and the imperial court. Some claim that he went to the Holy Land to study medicinal plants on the plains of Jericho, a topic he had lectured on before. Vesalius might have made a pilgrimage out of devotion, as did many millions before and after him. He planned to take a post at Padua upon his return, but he never reached Italy. He died on the island of Zenta off the Greek coast on October 15, 1564.

For More Information

Books

Finger, Stanley. *Minds Behind the Brain: The Pioneers and Their Discoveries.* New York: Oxford University Press, 2000.

Friedman, Meyer. *Medicine's 10 greatest Discoveries.* New Haven, Conn.: Yale University Press, 1998.

Web Sites

Ancient Medicine, from Homer to Vesalius. [Online] Available http://www.med.virginia.edu/hs-library/historical/antiqua/anthome.html, April 5, 2002.

Knight, Kevin. "Vesalius, Andreas." *Catholic Encyclopedia.* [Online] Available http://www.knight.org/advent/cathen/15378c.htm, April 5, 2002.

"Vesalius, Andreas." *Infoplease.com.* [Online] Available http://www.infoplease.com/ce5/CE054107.html, April 5, 2002.

Huldrych Zwingli

January 1, 1484
Wildhaus, Switzerland
October 11, 1531
Kappel, Switzerland

Religious reformer

Huldrych Zwingli.
Reproduced by permission of Archive Photos, Inc.

The Swiss Protestant reformer Huldrych Zwingli paved the way for the Protestant Reformation in Switzerland. (The Protestant Reformation was a reform movement that resulted in the establishment of a Christian religion separate from the Roman Catholic faith). Zwingli's ideas had a profound and long-lasting influence on church-state relations in Swiss cantons (states in the Swiss Confederation) that adopted Protestantism. A contemporary of **Martin Luther** (1483–1546; see entry), the German priest who initiated the Reformation, Zwingli made significant contributions that permanently affected Western (non-Asian) civilization.

Receives humanist education

Huldrych Zwingli was born on January 1, 1484, in the village of Wildhaus, Switzerland. He was one of ten children in a prosperous peasant family. His parents were determined that he should become a priest. In 1494 he was sent to school in Basel, Switzerland and in 1498 to Bern, Switzerland. During this time he was introduced to humanism, a literary and intellectual movement devoted to the revival of works by ancient Greek and Roman writers, which initiated the Renaissance. In 1500 Zwingli entered the University of Vienna in Austria to study philosophy. There he came into contact with such humanist scholars as Conradus Celtes (Conrad Pickle; 1459–1508). Zwingli also became an accomplished musician and played several instruments.

At the age of eighteen Zwingli was again in Basel, where he studied theology (religious philosophy and doctrines). In 1506 he received a master's degree and was ordained a priest by the bishop of Constance (the official who headed the church district based in Constance, Switzerland). Zwingli was then appointed parish priest at Glarus a few miles from his hometown of Wildhaus. He spent ten years in Glarus, a decade that was the most decisive period of his life. It was during this time that he developed his views as a reformer, his knowledge and love of Greek, his admiration for the great humanist **Desiderius Erasmus** (1466–1536; see entry), and his bitterness at the corruption in the church. Zwingli gained such an appreciation for pagan figures from Greek and Roman antiquity that he refused to believe that they were unredeemed because they had not known Christ. (It was a common belief that those who lived before the time of Jesus Christ, were not "saved" and therefore not in heaven.)

Begins questioning the church

In 1513 men from Glarus joined a unit in the army of Pope Leo X (1475–1521; reigned 1513–21), which was fighting in Italy against France on the side of Spain and the Holy Roman Empire. Zwingli went to Italy with the unit. After returning home, he recorded his impressions of the campaign in a fable (a story with animal characters that teaches a moral lesson) called *The Ox*. His message was that, for the security of the Swiss Confederation, it was essential not to sell out to foreign warlords. Rather, Switzerland should remain neutral in the power-plays of European wars. In 1515 the Swiss troops were defeated by the French in the Battle of Marignano. The following year, they signed a treaty with the French king **Francis I** (1494–1547; see entry), in which they agreed to sign up as mercenaries, or hired soldiers, in the French army—the former enemy—in exchange for economic benefits. When Zwingli's opposition to the treaty became public, he had to leave Glarus.

By 1516, when Zwingli moved to Einsiedeln in the canton of Schwyz, Switzerland, he was already questioning the church. He attacked such abuses as the sale of indulgences (partial forgiveness of sins) by priests to church members, and he criticized the spread of false relics (holy objects), such as pieces of the "True Cross" on which Jesus Christ was supposedly crucified, or locks of Jesus's baby hair. Zwingli also began to speak openly of a religion based only on the Bible (the Christian holy book). Independently of Martin Luther, he concluded that the papacy (office of the pope, the supreme head of the Roman Catholic Church) was unfounded in Scriptures (text of the Bible) and that church tradition did not have equal weight with the Bible as a source of Christian truth. Zwingli then spent three years as a priest at a Benedictine abbey (a monastery run by members of the Catholic order founded by Saint Benedict) in Einsiedeln. His experiences at Einsiedeln increased his dislike of selling indulgences. In addition to taking care of the spiritual needs of the small community, he preached to hundreds of pilgrims (those who go on religious journeys) who had come to do penance (confess their sins) and receive absolution (forgiveness of sins) by paying for indulgences. During his stay at the abbey, he devoted his time to classical studies. He also began reading a translation of the Bible published by Erasmus, which had a profound affect on him. Zwingli had been accustomed to reading the Bible commentaries of church "experts" instead of the text of the Bible itself, and his exposure to the Bible caused him to question the traditional interpretations of the Scripture.

By 1518 Zwingli's preaching skills had been noticed at the Great Minster, the main church in the city of Zurich. Late that year he eagerly accepted the offer to be the vicar, or people's priest, of the church. To better enable his audience to understand the word of God, in 1519 Zwingli began a series of lectures on the Gospel (message of Christ, considered the word of God) according to Saint Matthew (a book in the New Testament, the second part of the Bible). In his lectures he used simple terms and mentioned events in every day life. This was a radical approach because Catholic priests were considered authorities on the Bible and they were not allowed to help their parishioners interpret the Scripture. Despite some opposition from traditional priests, Zwingli's unusual method was soon adopted by his fellow priests at Great Minster.

Expresses revolutionary views

On March 5, 1522, in the home of the printer Christoph Froschauer (died 1564), some of Zwingli's friends and supporters broke the rule not eating meat during Lent by eating sausages. (Lent is a forty-day period prior to Easter, the celebration of Christ' rising from the dead. Christians devote this time to prayer, penance, and reflection. As a sign of fasting and additional penance, Catholics are not permitted to eat meat during Lent.) Zwingli turned this event into a public issue in his sermon, which he followed with a pamphlet. Not only did he support the actions of Froschauer and the others, but he also claimed that it was the right of every individual to choose freely what to eat.

The question of not eating meat during Lent triggered discussion of other issues, including clerical celibacy, the Catholic Church policy that does not permit priests to get married. Many clergymen of northern Switzerland were married, and Zwingli was among them. Secretly, he had married Anna Reinhart and had fathered several children. Together with ten other priests he sent a petition to the bishop of Constance asking for church recognition of their marriages. To strengthen their argument, they pointed out that the "bishops" (founders) of the early Church had also been married men. In addition, Zwingli took a stand against the veneration (worship) of saints (people declared as holy by the Catholic Church), and the practice of asking them for help and favors. Zwingli thought Christians could learn such qualities as humility, faith, and hope from the lives of the saints, but he believed in praying directly to God. Zwingli further questioned the belief that saints worked miracles. He had seen crowds of pilgrims flocking to shrines and praying for miracles, and he felt that the church was taking advantage of their faith to get rich. Zwingli contended that pictures and statues of saints only encouraged idolatry (worship of images, or false gods), so they should be taken down. Many of his most enthusiastic followers took his word literally, and from 1523 until 1525 they stripped decorations, statues, and pictures from all churches in Zurich. They frequently used violent tactics, causing disturbances in cantons that refused to adopt Zwingli's new methods.

In the sixteenth century, public debates (called disputations) were the generally accepted means for settling conflict. In January 1523 Zwingli invited the leading clergy of various cantons of the Swiss Confederation, including the bishop of Constance, to the Zurich town hall to discuss the recent issues. Most of his opponents refused to accept the invitation, and the bishop sent his personal adviser as an observer. Zwingli presented sixty-seven theses, (see accompanying box), which offered solutions to major problems in the church. Since the audience consisted mainly of his supporters, he easily convinced them to accept his plan. Zwingli's sixty-seven theses therefore became an outline for religious reform in Zurich. Among practices no longer considered acceptable were pilgrimages, processions, incense, noisy hymns, and the purchase of prayers and indulgences. Zwingli also advised his audience not to spend their money on such things as gambling and lavish clothing, but instead to use it to feed the poor and support widows and orphans. Additional reforms were decided upon at a second debate held later in the year. Among them were the closing of monasteries and the seizing of church property (land and wealth), which was to be given to the poor. The reformers also wanted to change the interpretation of communion (the ceremony in which bread and wine represent the body and blood of Christ). According to Catholic tradition, the bread and wine became the actual body and blood of Christ, a process called transubstantiation. Zwingli and his supporters contended, however, that communion had only symbolic significance, nothing more.

Zurich becomes evangelical city

During the years to come, Zwingli turned Zurich into an evangelical city. ("Evangelical" was a term used to refer to the reform movement in Germany.) Those who disagreed with Zwingli were forced either to comply or to leave. As early as 1524, some of Zwingli's supporters claimed his reforms did not go far enough. Among them were the Anabaptists, who formed their own movement called the Swiss Brethren. They were seen as a threat by the Zwinglians, who

Zwingli's Sixty-Seven Articles

In 1523 Huldrych Zwingli held a conference in Zurich to discuss reforms in the Roman Catholic Church. At the conference he presented sixty-five articles, or proposed reforms, which became the basis of the Reformation in Switzerland. Zwingli's sixty-seven articles became the basis for reform of the church in Zurich and, eventually, all of Switzerland.

Zwingli began the list with this statement:

> *I, Ulrich Zwingli, confess that I have preached in the worthy city of Zurich these sixty-seven articles or opinions on the basis of Scripture, which is called* theopneustos *(that is, inspired by God). I offer to defend and vindicate these articles with Scripture. But if I have not understood Scripture correctly, I am ready to be corrected, but only from the same Scripture.*

Zwingli touched on nearly every practice of the Catholic Church. In theses twenty-eight through thirty-three, he addressed the issues of marriage of priests (he himself was a married priest), excommunication, and the giving of unclaimed property to the church.

The Marriage of Clergy
28. Everything that God permits or has not forbidden is proper. From this we learn that marriage is proper for all people.

The Impure Priest Should Take a Wife
29. All those who are in the church sin if they do not make themselves secure through marriage once they understand that God has granted marriage to them for the sake of purity.

Vows of Purity
30. Those who take a vow of chastity assume madly or childishly too much. From this is to be learned that those who make such vows are treating godly people wantonly [recklessly].

Of Excommunication
31. No private person may excommunicate anyone else, but the church—that is, the communion of those among whom the one subject to excommunication lives—along with its guardians may act as a bishop.

32. The only one who should be excommunicated is a person who commits a public scandal.

Of Unclaimed Goods
33. Unclaimed goods should not be given to temples, cloisters, monks, priests, or nuns, but to the needy, if it is impossible to return them to their rightful owner.

Source: Mark A. Noll. Confessions and Catechisms of the Reformation. *Vancouver, B.C.: Regent College Publishing, 1997, pp. 42–43.*

Huldrych Zwingli's death at the Battle of Kappel in 1531.
©*Bettmann/Corbis.*
Reproduced by permission of Corbis Corporation.

banished Anabaptists from Zurich. In 1526 a Catholic-dominated conference was held in Baden, Switzerland. Zwingli was invited but he did not attend because he feared for his personal safety. The council condemned his reforms as the works of the "Antichrist [enemy of Christ] of the Great Minster."

On January 6, 1528, a disputation was allowed to take place in Bern, Switzerland. The debate lasted until the end of January, leaving no doubt that reforms Zwingli had demanded in Zurich would be carried out in the canton of Bern. One region, the Bernr Oberland, tried to resist, asking the neighboring states of Valais, Uri, and Unterwalden for spiritual and, eventually, military support. To reprimand the rebellious subjects, Bern sent in troops. The Bernr Oberland protestors soon gave up and accepted reforms. Zwingli had reached the summit of his power and influence. He had long dreamed of forming a Protestant Swiss Confederation (an alliance of cantons in Switzerland), but he needed the help of allies in Germany.

Zwingli dies in battle

Zwingli finally met Luther for the first time at a conference in Marburg, Germany, in 1529. The participants drew up fifteen articles that defined the Protestant faith. The Marburg meeting took place between the two Kappel Wars, religious conflicts between Catholics and Protestants. A truce was signed by both parties in 1529, but neither side seemed completely satisfied. When Zwingli returned home from the meeting, events seemed to develop in his favor. But shortly thereafter he met open resistance from the Catholic cantons, which were joined by opponents in his own ranks. Zwingli proposed a quick military campaign to put down opposition. Soon news reached Zurich that Catholic forces had gathered near Zug. Zurich's troops hurried in from all sides, but it was impossible to form orderly units on such short notice. Facing the well-prepared Catholic troops near Kappel in October 1531, the Protestant army of about fifteen hundred men fought bravely, but with no chance of victory. After only a few days, the Protestant alliance was defeated. Zurich lost about five hundred men in battle, among them its spiritual leader, Huldrych Zwingli. His body was abused by the victorious Catholics, who quartered it (cut it into four pieces) and burnt it on a heap of manure.

After Zwingli's death, his colleague Heinrich Bullinger (1504–1575) became the pastor at Great Minster and the leader of the reform movement in Switzerland. In 1536 Bullinger played an important role in compiling the First Helvetic Confession, a statement of reform goals based largely on Zwingli's views. In 1549 Bullinger joined the French reformer **John Calvin** (1509–1564; see entry) in drafting the Consensus of Tigurnius, which moved Swiss reform efforts toward Calvinism (a strict form of Protestantism).

For More Information

Books
Gäbler, Ulrich. *Huldrych Zwingli: His Life and Work*. Ruth C. L. Gritsch, translator. Philadelphia: Fortress Press, 1986.

Web Sites
Protestant Reformation. [Online] Available http://www.mun.ca/rels/hroll mann/reform/reform.html, April 5, 2002.

"Zwingli, Ulrich." *Encyclopedia.com.* [Online] Available http://www. encyclopedia.com/searchpool.asp?target=@DOCTITLE%20Zwingli% 20%20Huldreich%20or%20Ulrich, April 5, 2002.

"Zwingli, Ulrich." *Zwingli and Luther.* [Online] Available http://www. bible.org/docs/history/schaff/vol7/schaf176.htm, April 5, 2002.

Index

Italic type indicates volume numbers. **Bold** type indicates main entries and their page numbers. Illustrations are marked by (ill.)

T

U

V

W

Z